hands on art

D0522898

Brenda Whittle

Acknowledgments

The author and publisher would like to thank the children of Bushfield Road Infant School, Priory Lane Infant School, Bottesford Infant School and St Francis Community Special School for their wonderful artwork.

The author would like to give very special thanks to the following people for their creative ideas, expertise and support in making the production of this book possible:

The staff at Bushfield Road Infant School, in particular head teacher Liz Carr, art co-ordinator Karen Turnbull, teachers Tracy Bass, Pam Lloyd, Janine Burnham, Bernadette Sharp, Sarah Miller and Jayne Mason.

Teachers Emma Cryne and Julia Portas of Priory Lane Infant School and head teacher Sue White.

Rachel Dalgairns of Bottesford Infant School.

Bo Meacher and Ralph Carter of St Francis Community Special School.

Patchwork Patterns (page 50)

First published in 2007 by Belair Publications.
Apex Business Centre, Boscombe Road, Dunstable, LU5 4RL

Belair publications are protected by international copyright laws. All rights reserved.

The copyright of all materials in this publication, except where otherwise stated, remains the property of the publisher and author. No part of this publication may be reproduced, stored in a retrieval system, or transmitted, in any form or by any means, for whatever purpose, without the written permission of Belair Publications.

Brenda Whittle hereby asserts her moral right to be identified as the author of this work in accordance with the Copyright, Designs and Patents Act 1988.

Commissioning Editor: Zoë Nichols   Editor: Sara Wiegand
Design: Philippa Jarvis   Photography: Roger Brown and Steve Forest

Cover design: Steve West

© 2007 Folens on behalf of the author.

Every effort has been made to trace the copyright holders of material used in this publication. If any copyright holder has been overlooked, we should be pleased to make the necessary arrangements.

British Library Cataloguing in Publication Data. A catalogue record for this publication is available from the British Library.

ISBN 1-84191-450-9

Contents

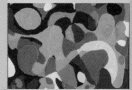

Introduction

Cross-curricular approach

This book takes a cross-curricular approach to the teaching of art to young children in order to make art relevant and an integral part of the curriculum. Art is relevant to every area of the curriculum. It provides ready-made opportunities for children to be a little more observant and a little more creative. This book has been compiled with the help of practitioners who are all committed to ensuring that the children they teach have the opportunity to enjoy a wide variety of art experiences.

Developing creativity

Teachers need to provide stimulating starting points for art which give children the freedom to think for themselves and the time to develop their own creativity. After many years in teaching, and with a love of teaching art in primary schools, I have come to the conclusion that creativity is innate in all children. Children have a natural desire to try things out and to express themselves, but their confidence in their own creativity can be fragile and requires careful nurturing.

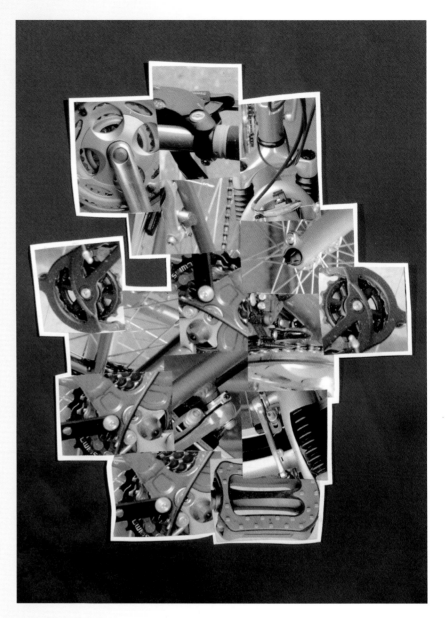

Children need to feel that they have succeeded in their art work in order to gain the confidence to push their creative boundaries a little further and take a few risks. A part of feeling confident in their abilities means accepting that sometimes their art work will not turn out in the way they wanted; but this is just part of the process of learning and developing and not a sign of failure. It is therefore important that teachers plan activities in which all children can feel confident in their own achievement. Children want to be looking, thinking, talking, doing and reflecting. I cannot remember ever teaching a child who did not enjoy art work, if he or she completed it with a sense of achievement.

Activities and displays

The activities in this book are grouped in chapters, but inevitably an activity in one chapter is likely to have close links with another chapter. For example, when looking at pattern, you are very likely to be also talking about colour and shape. Each activity outlines ideas for art work that can be used to produce a display and contains three more related art activities. These are followed by activities linked to three other areas of the curriculum. You may decide to follow a complete activity or just take sections or ideas from it, adapting them to fit in with a theme you have planned. The display ideas can be used as a complete step-by-step guide or as a starting point for the practitioner, who may use elements from them and adapt and change them to be relevant in a particular setting.

Required skills

Many different skills are required for the activities in this book. If children do not already have the relevant skills, these will need to be taught first. It is worth spending a few moments before the start of any activity reminding children of even the simplest skills, such as how to mix colours, how to use glue effectively or how to sew a running stitch. The results will be more rewarding for the children if they are using the appropriate skills.

Safety first

Particular care should be taken to follow safety rules and to check for allergies when working outside, asking children to touch plants and seeds or involving them in the tasting of foods.

Making a start

Whether you are reading this book because you already love teaching art or in order to try to find inspiration in a subject you feel unsure about, remember that you hold the key to your children's success. It is within your power to provide the environment and opportunities that they need in order to develop their creative selves. Start by introducing an activity that inspires you and then you will find that your enthusiasm and genuine delight in the children's achievements will be a recipe for success.

Brenda Whittle

My Life

First I was a baby ...... then I was a toddler ... then I went to playgroup now we are at school.

Starting points

- Ask the children to think about the main stages of their lives so far. Choose four stages such as baby, toddler, starting playgroup and starting school. Discuss how they have changed since they were babies. Talk about the physical changes and changes in the types of clothes they have worn.

- Ask the children to list items that are appropriate to each stage. These might include objects such as a rattle and nappy for the baby stage and paint pot, paintbrush, bucket and spade for the playgroup stage. Make a collection of these items.

Display

1. Collect four cardboard or plastic boxes of equal size to form the basis of the display. Cardboard boxes could be painted inside and out. One group of children can be responsible for choosing, creating and displaying the contents of each box, depicting one particular stage of their lives.

2. Ask the children to bring in photographs of themselves at the chosen stage for example, when they were toddlers. Ask them to look carefully at the photograph and draw a picture of themselves wearing the same clothes against the same background. Choose one of these drawings to display in a frame. The children can make their own labels using a word processor and display the collection of items appropriate to that stage.

3. Ask each child in the class to produce a drawing of their face. Cut out the faces and display as a montage in a photograph frame beside the final 'now we are at school' display box.

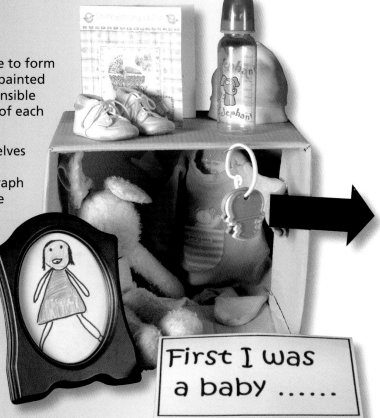

First I was a baby ......

Further activities

- Ask the children to make a collection of images of children portrayed in different media, which could include their own family albums, magazines and advertisements. Display these and give the children time to examine and talk about them.

- Look at portraits of children painted by different artists and discuss the background and items included in each picture. Tell the children that you are going to produce a portrait of each of them in the form of a photograph. Ask the children to think about things they enjoy doing in school, items they would choose to include in their portrait and where they would choose the photograph to be taken. Older children may be able to photograph each other. If using a digital camera, the photographs can be made into a slideshow for the children to access.

- Ask the children to think of someone who is special in their lives and to make a line drawing of that person, using a black felt-tipped pen. Mount the drawings in a circle to show the class's 'special people'.

Cross-curricular links

SCIENCE – Ask the children to think about how they have grown taller and changed since they were born and whether the tallest person in the class is necessarily the oldest. Ask them to speculate about how tall they think they will grow and what they will look like as adults. Help the children to measure their height using non-standard measures, such as yogurt pots or hands. As some children may be sensitive about their height, encourage children to be sensitive to the differences between them.

NUMERACY – Talk about the ways in which we all look different from each other. Start by comparing eye and hair colour. Begin to collect data about the children in the class and introduce the idea of showing that data in different forms. For example you could compare eye colour and show this data in the form of a model, using cubes to show the number of children with each eye colour, make a pictogram or use a simple graphs program on the computer.

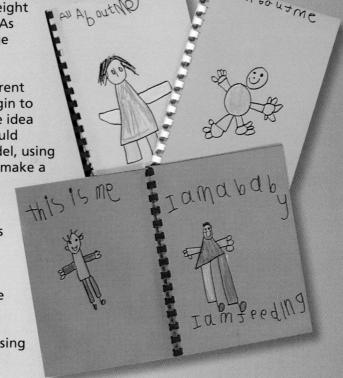

LITERACY – Write 'All about me' on a board or large sheet of paper and ask the children to tell you some of the things they can do. Talk about how long the list is and how much they have achieved in their lives. Provide each child with a booklet containing six sheets. They can draw a picture of themselves on the cover, with the title 'All about me'. Write 'I can…' at the top of each page and ask the children to draw a picture showing something they can do, adding the appropriate text. Use the finished books as an aid to increasing the children's self-esteem.

My School and Me

Starting points

- Talk about being in school and the places, events and people that are important to the children during the school day. Narrow the list down to about four headings, for example: 'In my classroom', 'My lunch and snack', 'In my playground' and 'My friends'.

- Read stories and poems about school. Talk about the activities that the children enjoy doing inside and outside the classroom and list their likes and dislikes.

- In circle time, talk about friends and how important they are to us. Ask the children to think about who their friends are and discuss why it is important that they all try to be friends with each other.

Display

1. Use four boxes as the basis of the display. Paint the boxes inside and out and make labels for each one (suggested headings as above). Use the boxes to house the children's collections of chosen items.

2. For the 'In my classroom' box, collect items to represent different classroom activities, for example: a pencil drawing, a painting, a model, a drawing completed on the computer, a favourite story book, a spade from the sand tray, a pair of scissors and some building bricks.

3. For the 'My lunch and snack' box, the children can make the contents of a lunch box, a school lunch and a snack using dough. These dough models can be dried out by cooking slowly and can then be painted and varnished. Make and laminate labels for each model. Ask the children to match the labels to the foods.

4. The 'In my playground' box could contain: a skipping rope, a ball, 'small world' items such as a bicycle, pram, or scooter and photographs of the children playing outside.

5. The 'My friends' box could include a tape of the children talking. Ask each child to contribute by saying, 'My name is… I like …'. The children can draw pictures of themselves taking part in their favourite activities, adding their names at the bottom, and then these pictures can be cut out and laminated. When children take these pictures out of the box to play with, they can stand the figures up by pushing the base of each into modelling material.

Further activities

- Provide mirrors and ask the children, and any adults working in the classroom, to look at their reflections in a mirror and then draw or paint a picture of themselves. Cut out the pictures. Make a large circle from coloured paper and mount the drawings around the edge, saving one to use in the centre. Make a speech bubble for the picture of the child in the centre, asking, 'Who is my friend?' At the top of the display, in the centre, add the words 'We are!' (see page 8).

- Ask the children to pair up with a friend and use chalks to draw a picture of each other on a paved area outside. Show the children that they need to press hard to produce blocks of stronger colour and can achieve paler effects by pressing lightly. Use these drawings as a talking point, showing that everyone has a friend.

Cross-curricular links

SCIENCE – Talk about the fact that we need food and drink to keep us healthy and help us grow. Ask the children to think about healthy snacks that they could eat at break time. Include items such as fruits and vegetables and water or milk to drink. Tell the children that you are going to choose five items together that they can all taste for their snacks the following week. Try to choose some foods which you think they may not have tried. Make a list together showing the day of the week and the type of snack planned for that day. Encourage the children to try the snacks and talk about their likes and dislikes.

NUMERACY – At the end of the week when the children taste the different snacks, show them how to record their likes and dislikes. Ask the children to decide which of the five choices is their favourite. Make a 3-D record by asking each child to record the snack of their choice on a block graph, using real fruits. Discuss their findings.

PHYSICAL DEVELOPMENT – Ask the children to think about the skills they have which involve using their hands in classroom activities. These could include: cutting, painting, writing, manipulating building bricks, pouring water or filling containers with sand. Focus on cutting skills and ask the children to draw lines and cut along them, or draw simple shapes and cut these out. Include pinking scissors that cut in a variety of patterns.

Look at Me!

Starting points

- Explain to the children what is meant by a portrait and a self-portrait. Provide a range of examples of reproductions of portraits and self-portraits by famous artists for the children to look at.

- Ask the children to sit opposite a partner and look carefully at each other's faces, noticing the face shape, features, skin colour, hair texture and colour.

- Provide a range of drawing media such as charcoal, pencils, pastels and fine black felt-tipped pens. Ask the children to experiment with making marks in a sketch book or on a sheet of paper to draw parts of their partner's face or hair. Emphasise that these are experiments and encourage the children to try out a range of ideas and techniques.

Display

1. Ask the children to look at their faces in mirrors and to tell you if their faces are flat. Ask them to run their fingers over their faces, noticing which parts stick out, such as the nose and which parts are sunken, such as the eye sockets.

2. Explain to the children that you want them to use the information that they have found out and to work together to make two large models of faces. Wooden boards or strong pieces of cardboard make suitable bases for the children to form the outline of the face and features by gluing down scrunched-up newspaper in the shape they require. When the outline and features are in place, show the children how to cover these with wet plaster bandages which give a hard surface when dry. When thoroughly dry, the face can be painted and varnished.

3. Display the faces on a board. Provide oil pastels or paints and ask the children to draw faces and use these as a border around the display. After looking at body shapes (see 'Further activities'), make figures using string glued onto black paper and add these to the display. Look at faces painted by Pablo Picasso and ask the children to draw faces in the style of one of his paintings and incorporate these drawings into the display.

Further activities

- Explain to the children that you want them to make a portrait of a fictitious character using recycled materials. Provide a wide range of materials such as plastic containers, bottle tops, lids, cardboard tubes and packaging. Explain that they are free to make the portrait in any way they choose. Use cardboard, wood or hardboard as a base for the work. The recycled objects can be glued to the base, and the portrait could be incorporated into the main display.

- During a P.E. lesson, ask the children to be aware of the different shapes they can make with their bodies, transferring their weight onto different parts of their bodies and holding each shape steady. Take photographs with a digital camera and use these photos for reference. Provide the children with clay or pipe cleaners and ask them to look at the photographs of their body shapes and to make figures which reflect the variety of positions. Involve the children in the creation of a 3-D park scene in which to display the figures.

- Ask the children to take photographs of each other over the period of a day: arriving at school, in the classroom, in the playground or eating lunch. Print the photographs and use these to make a montage of their day.

Cross-curricular links

DESIGN AND TECHNOLOGY – Visit a local playground and encourage the children to have fun on the equipment, after making clear the safety rules they should follow. Discuss with the children the types of equipment and ask them to make drawings and take photographs of these. Encourage them to take notes on the different materials from which the pieces of equipment are built and how the different parts are joined together. Back in the classroom, the children can refer to their photographs, drawings and notes and use everyday items such as straws, tape, pipe cleaners and construction kits to make 3-D models of play equipment.

PSHCE – Ask the children if they can tell how someone is feeling by looking at their face. Talk about emotions that can be displayed in facial features such as feeling happy, sad or scared. Sit in a circle with the children and ask them to 'pass on' to the next person the emotion you are showing with your face.

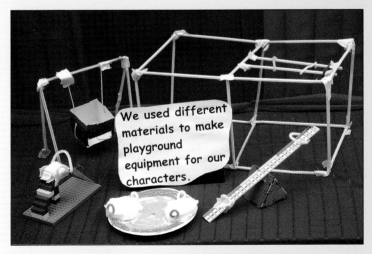

P.E. – Talk about the importance of keeping healthy and the part that exercise plays in feeling good. During P.E. activities, ask the children to tell you which parts of their bodies they are exercising. Ask them to describe how they feel during and after exercise, identifying that they may feel hotter, tired or thirsty after exercising.

Hands Up!

Starting points

- Ask the children to look at their hands and compare their size, skin colour and shape with each other. Encourage them to look at the lines and skin on their palms and the shape of their nails.

- Have they noticed that older people's hands look different from theirs? If possible, arrange for a parent to bring in a baby so that the children can look at a baby's hands.

- Talk about decorations we might wear on our hands, for example rings, bracelets or mendhi patterns.

Display

1. Invite the children to use powder paint to try to mix the colour of the skin on their hands. When mixing paint for a white skin, remind the children that a little yellow added to very pale pink paint will give a more natural result.

2. Provide cartridge paper and ask the children to look carefully at one of their hands and make a drawing of it about 20cm long. They can then paint it with the colour they have already mixed.

3. If a mix of skin colours is not represented in the children in the class, talk about other skin colours and paint hands in these colours. Cut out the hands and staple to the display board in the shape of one large hand.

Further activities

- Cut large hand shapes from stiff card and tape to pieces of dowelling. Push the dowelling into modelling material. Create rings from strips of card painted gold or silver to fit the fingers on the hand. Ask the children to decorate the rings using beads, foil or sequins.

- Show the children examples of mendhi patterns drawn on hands. Make oval shapes in play dough, slightly larger than a child's hand. Cut around the hand shape using a clay tool. Make a hole in the bottom of the play dough hand for a lollipop stick. Dry the dough in an oven at a low temperature. When cool, paint the hands and add mendhi patterns using felt-tipped pens. Display on the lollipop stands pushed into modelling material.

- Take the opportunity to discuss sensitively the fact that everybody's skin colour is unique to them and there are many different colours. Ask the children to compare skin colours within the class, or through books and pictures, and ask them to experiment in mixing the different colours they see to make a montage.

Cross-curricular links

PSHCE – Talk about families and discuss how all families are different. Ask the children to think about the people who make up their families and encourage them to make finger puppets showing some of the members of their families. Demonstrate how to make the basic finger puppet shape from cartridge paper and draw in the features. The children can add hair made from wool, paper or string. Spectacles, hats or scarves can also be added.

NUMERACY – Make a hand matching game. Ask the children to draw and cut out hand shapes from brightly coloured paper. Photocopy and cut out the copies of each hand shape and stick them at varying angles onto an A3-sized base board. Laminate the base. Glue a piece of Velcro to the centre of each hand on the board. Laminate each of the coloured hand shapes and attach a piece of Velcro to its underside (checking that it matches exactly with its 'partner' on the baseboard). Attach the baseboard to a wall and put the coloured hands in a box. The children can then match the hands to those on the wall.

MUSIC – Experiment with making different sounds using the hands, for example: clapping, rubbing them together, rubbing the nails together, clicking or tapping two fingers on the palm. Make a simple rhythm using one or more of these sounds and ask the children to copy it.

It's Party Time!

Starting points

- Talk about celebrations in the children's lives. Discuss how and why people celebrate events such as birthdays, weddings, Christmas or Divali.
- Tell the children that they are going to plan and prepare a party for everyone in the class to share. Ask them to think about what is needed to make a party and write a list together. Include food, drinks, music, invitations and decorations.
- Decide together on a colour theme for the party such as 'hot colours', 'gold and silver' or 'the rainbow'.

Display

1. Make a collection of birthday invitations and talk about the design and layout of these with the children. Make a giant-sized invitation card as the basis of the display. Fold in half a piece of fairly thick card approximately 90cm x 60cm.

2. Talk about the ways in which you can make a dramatic effect with a simple design such as an explosion of colour, or 'sunburst' effect, to give a lively and exciting party feel. Ask the children to experiment, painting sunbursts using thick paint in shades of the chosen party theme colours. Choose one of the designs and ask the children to paint this design on the large invitation card which forms the basis of the display. Represent party music with musical notes cut from black paper.

3. Play party music and ask the children to join hands in a line and dance around the room. Ask them to 'freeze' when the music stops and to look at the position of their bodies. After this activity, ask each child to draw themselves in their party clothes, with arms outstretched as though they were dancing in a line. Cut out the finished drawings and glue them together to make a line of children. You could cut a 'doorway' in the left-hand side of the card and make the line of children dance their way through the door and across the card. Pin or glue the figures in place.

Further activities

- Discuss the items needed for a party such as plastic cups, tablecloths and paper napkins. Suggest that the children print sunburst designs onto white paper tablecloths and napkins, using the same colour theme as in the display. Provide pieces of thick card and let the children experiment with making sunburst designs of different sizes by pressing the edges of card into thick paint and printing onto the tablecloths and napkins.

- Discuss the types of food the children would like to serve at the party. Suggest making miniature examples of the foods they want to use out of play dough and setting out a sample tray of party food. Bake the play dough food at a low temperature and paint and varnish when cold. Arrange on a plate and put the plate on a tray covered with one of the printed napkins. Print a paper cup with the theme design and add to the tray.

- Talk about party games which children played in the past (see 'Cross-curricular links' – History), in particular Pin the Tail on the Donkey. Ask the children to adapt this game using their own ideas, for example: Land the Rocket on the Moon, Put the Baby in the Pram or Put Father Christmas on the Chimney. Ask the children to work with a partner, designing and drawing the background on a piece of A3-sized card. Draw and cut out the character or object needed to play the game. Play the games and talk about which ones the class like, and why.

Can you pin the rocket on the moon ?

Cross-curricular links

LITERACY – Make a collection of menus from cafés and restaurants and look at their content, design, colour and the style of lettering used. Ask the children to list the food they want to serve at their party and decide on the style and layout of a menu to encourage their guests to try the different foods. Children can work with a partner, producing their own menus decorated in the same style and colour theme as the other party items.

DESIGN AND TECHNOLOGY – Talk about the importance of fruit and vegetables in our diet. Ask the children to think about the ways in which they could arrange a plate of pieces of fruit or vegetables, using the sunburst theme, so that it would look appealing and provide a healthy snack. Remind children of the importance of hygiene and following safety procedures when preparing food and using kitchen utensils.

HISTORY – Ask the children to talk about the parties they go to and the activities they enjoy. Play some traditional party games, for example: Musical Chairs, Hide and Seek, Pass the Parcel, Charades and Pin the Tail on the Donkey. Ask the children to compare these games with the activities they enjoy at parties.

Move It

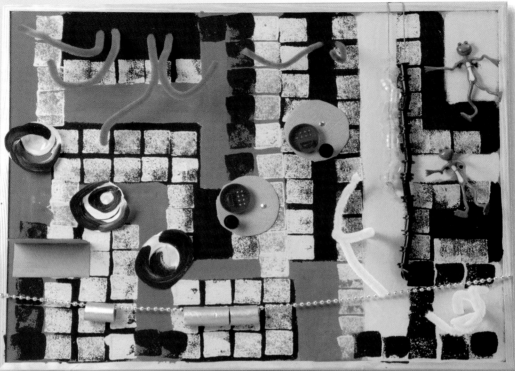

Starting points

- Make a collection of things that have interesting moving parts, for example: a baby's cot play centre, a key in a padlock, a spring or a beaded door hanging.

- Give the children time to explore and enjoy playing with the objects. Listen to their comments and ask questions about how the different parts move and what sounds they make when they are moving.

- Explain to the children that they are going to make a 'Move It' board. The display board will need to be at child height so that the children can stand in front of it to touch and move the items they make.

Display

1. Make a collection of materials, such as: metal or plastic lids, springs, pipe cleaners, keys and padlocks, coloured Cellophane, card, wooden beads, decorative bells, elastic, boxes and tubes.

2. Divide the display board into sections and ask the children to paint or print each section. Let them try out their ideas for making objects with moving parts to display on the board.

3. They could:
   - make circular spinners from card painted in patterns and then attached to a piece of card using a split pin through the centre.
   - thread large wooden beads onto laces and hang from the board.
   - attach objects to springs so that they will move up and down when touched.
   - attach padlocks to the board, with the corresponding keys hanging from string.
   - staple pieces of card along one side to make doors which open and close.
   - add a box with a hole cut in the top and rubber bands pulled across the hole.

Further activities

- Choose a rhyme that gives scope to make one or more moving parts when illustrating it, such as 'Hickory Dickory Dock'. Ask a child to draw a grandfather clock on a piece of card and write the rhyme at the side. Draw the clock face and add the numbers. Attach some hands with a paper fastener so that they can move round and round. Make a mouse from card and secure to the base of the clock with Velcro. When the children move the hands to one o'clock, they move the mouse up the clock.

- Ask the children to draw wide stripes, along the length of a piece of cartridge paper or card and then paint the stripes using two colours. Cut along the stripes, to approximately 2cm from the ends. Cut several strips of paper at least twice as long as the width of the painted paper and paint these in stripes along the width using the same colours. Weave the strips into the backing paper. The children can move the strips to create different designs.

- Collect old CDs and encourage the children to notice their reflective properties. Ask the children to draw a design based on a circle on the CD using oil pastels. They could draw concentric circles or lines radiating from the centre. Hang the CDs from a piece of cane to produce a mobile that catches the light.

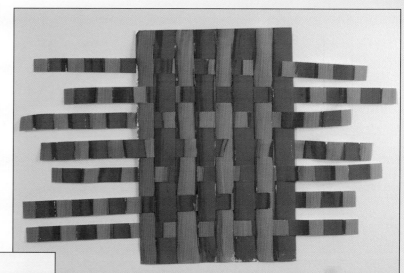

The wheels on the bus go round and round......

Cross-curricular links

MUSIC – Make a collection of objects that could be used to make simple rubber-band guitars, such as assorted boxes, empty tins with the lids removed or pieces of plastic guttering. Show the children how to stretch rubber bands of assorted thicknesses over these items and pluck them to make sounds. Decorate the guitars by covering them with paper or papier mache and then painting them. Give the children time to try out their guitars and talk about the different sounds they can make.

SCIENCE – Provide a collection of musical instruments such as guiros, tambourines, maracas and triangles and encourage the children to experiment in making sounds.

NUMERACY – Ask one child to draw and paint a bus with large windows, but no wheels, as these will be made separately. Other children can draw and paint the driver's and passengers' faces to cut out and place on the windows. Laminate the bus on A3-sized card. Paint, cut out and laminate five large wheels and attach these to the bus with split pins through the centre so that they will turn round. Paint the numbers 1–5 below the wheels. The children can sing the song 'The Wheels on the Bus' as they turn the wheels.

Stories and Rhymes

Starting points

- Make a collection of traditional story or rhyme books which could also be used as starting points to encourage counting. These could include stories and rhymes, such as: 'Goldilocks and the Three Bears', 'The Three Little Pigs', 'Snow White and the Seven Dwarfs', 'One, Two, Three, Four, Five' and 'One, Two, Buckle my Shoe'.

- Choose a well-illustrated copy of the story of 'Goldilocks and the Three Bears' and read it to the children. After talking about the story, ask the children to act out the story as you tell or read the narrative. Talk about the characters' appearance, where the story is set and the sequence of events.

- Show the children the illustrations in the book. Make a collection of items similar to those in the pictures for the children to touch and feel. These could include bricks, tiles, bark, leaves and teddy bears. Encourage the children to describe the textures using adjectives such as smooth, rough, soft, hard, squashy, furry or shiny.

Display

1. Make a scene from the story showing the wood, the bears and the bears' house. Ask the children to think about the colours they would see in a wood, such as shades of green and brown for the vegetation, and then paint or sponge print the background. On separate sheets of paper, ask the children to draw and cut out trees, the three bears, and the bears' house.

2. Provide a selection of textured fabrics, papers (including sandpaper and corrugated card), bubble wrap, and recycled materials for the children to choose from and use in the picture. Glue or staple the bears, trees and house to the background. Ask the children to choose other things to add to the picture such as animals, flowers or birds.

3. Ask the children to think about what they would see through the windows of the bears' house, such as the table set with three bowls of porridge. Discuss together and set up a simple role play for the scenes, which the children can then photograph. Print the photographs and glue them in the window spaces.

Further activities

- Choose a rhyme that gives scope for including a tree in a display, such as 'Dive Little Froggies' or 'What's the Time, Mr Wolf?' Go for a 'tree' walk in the local environment. Ask the children to look at and feel the texture of the tree trunks and observe the colours they see in the branches, trunks and leaves. As part of the display, make a tree showing the different textures and colours using fabrics, threads and stitches. Glue or sew the tree to a coarse fabric, such as hessian.

- Read the children the traditional story of 'The Three Little Pigs'. Collect straw, bricks and pieces of wood. Check first that the materials are safe to handle and then let the children feel them and talk about the different textures of the materials. Discuss with the children how you can plan a picture together showing the three different houses. They will have their own ideas, but they could draw the three houses and glue straw to one, wooden lollipop sticks to another and cut out brick shapes from sandpaper for the third.

- Read the children the story of 'Little Red Riding Hood'. Use this as a starting point to encourage them to think about colour and texture. Provide some red fabric to represent Red Riding Hood's cape and ask the children to choose red items from a collection of fabric scraps, magazines, wools and papers and display these on the fabric. The display will provide the opportunity to talk about the different textures of the materials and the fact that there are many different shades of red.

Cross-curricular links

LITERACY – Ask the children to consider which additional materials might have been used to make the brick house in the story of 'The Three Little Pigs'. These could include wood for the doors and window frames, glass for the windows, tiles for the roof as well as the bricks for the walls. Show the children how to find information about materials in books or CD-ROMs.

NUMERACY – Teach the children the rhyme 'Ten Green Bottles' to help them understand the concept of subtraction. Make a simple display by cutting bottle shapes from thick card and covering each with a different type of green material, which could include plastic, fur fabric, painted twigs, sponge pieces, string or metal washers. The children can remove the bottles as they sing the rhyme.

SCIENCE – After exploring which materials are attracted to magnets, ask the children to make a set of fridge magnets, illustrating the rhyme 'Five Little Ducks Went Swimming One Day'. Draw, colour and cut out the ducks and glue to magnets.

Natural and Reclaimed

Starting points

- If possible, arrange a visit to a wood, park or coastal area. Make a collection of natural materials such as seed heads, leaves, bark, shells and pebbles, ensuring that the children only collect materials which have fallen or are dead. When collecting any materials, make sure that children follow health and safety rules.

- Make a collection of reclaimed materials such as cardboard boxes, plastic containers, shredded paper and bubble wrap. (Children should not handle glass objects.)

- Ask the children to look at the shapes, colours and textures of the materials, describing them as they do so.

Display

1. Ask the children to choose a simple symmetrical shape such as a circle and draw this shape on card, with the circle measuring approximately one metre in diameter. Draw a line dividing the shape in half, start arranging the reclaimed materials in patterns on one side and echo the pattern in natural materials on the opposite side. When the pattern is established, glue the pieces in place.

2. The children could make a border for the display on the 'natural' side by tying black thread around twigs and attaching them to the display board. Glue or staple a collection of small containers such as yogurt pots, boxes and lids to make a border on the 'reclaimed' side.

3. Add a basket of natural materials and a plastic bowl or cardboard box of reclaimed materials for the children to handle and discuss.

Further activities

- Show the children examples of reproductions of Aboriginal art where the designs are based on circles. Make collections of reclaimed or natural materials and give the children time to experiment freely in arranging them on a board to create a design in a similar style. Glue the materials in place.

- Extend the work by looking at Aboriginal art designs that show circles inside circles. Provide a hessian backing, fabrics, threads and beads in natural colours to enable the children to create a wall hanging based on circles. Experiment with textures by weaving circles on card looms and adding beads or shells to give a 3-D effect.

- Show the children pictures of the work of Andy Goldsworthy and explain that his sculptures may be temporary. Arrange a visit to a park, wood or seaside and ask the children to collect natural materials that they can use 'in situ' to make their own sculptures. Photograph their work.

Cross-curricular links

SCIENCE – Provide a collection of materials and ask the children to sort them into those which are found in nature and those which are not, or ask the children to sort the materials according to their own criteria.

LITERACY – Ask the children to work with a partner, labelling the natural objects they have found. Glue objects such as a shell, leaf or seed head to a piece of card, and write the name below it.

PSHCE – Talk about the importance of keeping safe when collecting materials in the environment. Discuss with the children the reasons why they should not touch glass or sharp objects and why they must avoid areas contaminated with dog faeces. Remind children of the importance of washing their hands after collecting and handling materials and explain the reasons why. Talk about the importance of conserving our environment and not damaging plants or disturbing areas when they are collecting dead or fallen materials.

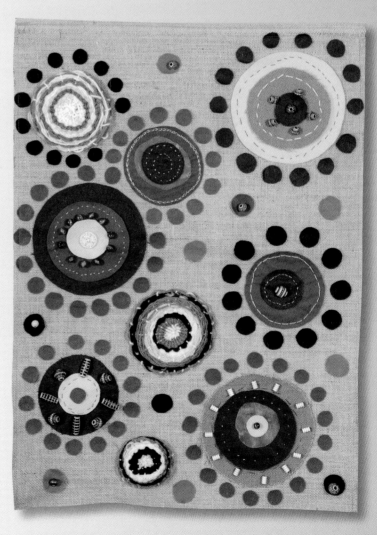

Birds

Starting points

- Provide food on a bird table or in hanging feeders to attract birds. Talk to the children about the types of food that birds eat, showing them different types of nuts, seeds and fruits.

- Talk about the size, colour and shape of the birds they see and ask the children to make observational drawings or paintings. If possible take photographs of the birds for the children to refer to when drawing. Provide books and help them to identify the different birds.

- Talk to the children about the ways in which birds find their food, other than from foods which we provide. Explain that birds eat growing plants and fruits from gardens or fields and that sometimes people make bird scarers such as scarecrows to frighten them away and save their crops.

Display

1. Teach the children rhymes about scarecrows such as 'Dingle Dangle Scarecrow' or 'I'm a Little Scarecrow'. Show them pictures of crows and scarecrows. Explain to the children that you want them to make their own scarecrows.

2. Provide straw, lollipop sticks, thin card and fabrics such as hessian and felt. Show the children how to make a simple scarecrow by gluing a triangle of hessian onto a lollipop stick and adding a face made from card. Add a felt hat and straw for the arms and hair.

3. Ask a child to draw and cut out a large scarecrow. Glue on pieces of fabric for the clothes and straw for the head, hands and feet. Complete the figure with a hat and scarf. Refer to the pictures of crows and ask the children to paint crows to use in their display. Decide together which crop is growing in the field or garden and paint the appropriate plants.

Further activities

- Teach the children 'Sing a Song of Sixpence' and role play the actions. Tell the children that you want them to make a large picture to illustrate the song. Find pictures of blackbirds and ask the children to refer to these before painting and cutting out twenty-four blackbirds for the picture. Paint and cut out a large pie. Glue the paintings onto backing paper.

- Show the children pictures of peacocks and talk about the colours and patterns in their tails. Ask a child to draw a peacock's body and suggest that they all help to make the tail. Ask the children each to make a handprint using green paint. When this is dry, make another print on top in a different colour, by painting a circle on the base of the palm of the hand. Make a third print by painting a spiral on the hand in another colour. Cut out the handprints and use to make the peacock's tail.

- Secure a small branch in a pot to use as a tree. Provide card, beads, glue, felt-tipped pens and collage materials such as foils, papers and Cellophane. Ask the children to draw and cut out a bird shape in card and to add collage materials and beads to make a fantasy bird. Attach the birds to the branch with glue or thread.

Cross-curricular links

SCIENCE – Observe birds in the local environment or by looking at pictures and photographs. Name the different parts of a bird's body. Ask the children to draw a picture of a bird and point to, or label, the different parts of the body. Give the children the opportunity to observe the great variety of birds throughout the world by using books, pictures or the internet.

LITERACY – Read or tell traditional stories to the children such as 'The Little Red Hen', 'The Ugly Duckling' and 'Chicken Licken'. Ask one or two children to re-tell the stories, with the rest of the group role-playing the different parts.

Lots of Leaves

- Go on a walk looking at leaves and the different shapes and sizes of trees, shrubs and plants. Take photographs and use reference books to identify the plants and trees when back in the classroom.

- Make a collection of leaves of differing shapes, colours and sizes. Ask the children to use their senses when examining the leaves. If possible, include some leaves such as mint or basil, so that the children notice the smell as well as the colour and texture. Compare the underside of the leaf with the top and point out the veins and edges.

- Ask the children to work with a partner and make a picture of a face using only leaves. Talk about their pictures and photograph them.

Display

1. Talk to the children about the ways in which they could make leaf shapes using modelling material such as play dough or clay. Ask them to work with a partner and choose a leaf from the collection and mould the clay into the same shape, particularly noticing details such as the veins and whether the edges are smooth or serrated. The moulded leaves should be about 6–8cm long. Draw in the veins using a modelling tool or pencil. When happy with the design, the moulded leaves can be baked on a low heat. You will need several different leaf shapes for the display.

2. Explain to the children that you want them to use their leaves to create one design together. Discuss the colours of leaves at different times of the year. Encourage the children to mix greens, reds, oranges, yellows and browns and then paint and varnish the leaves.

3. Ask the children to experiment with arranging the leaves in different ways on a piece of board or thick cardboard. They can incorporate twigs or artificial berries into the design. Give the children time to try out different ideas. When they are happy with their design, glue the leaves onto the board.

Further activities

- Discuss with the children the types of birds and animals they might see in trees, such as owls or squirrels. Explain that you want them to use leaf shapes to make a bird or animal using fabric, threads and stitching to create the effect. An owl would be an ideal choice as the leaves can be used for the feathers and the large eyes are achieved by weaving around circles of card. Cut the leaves out of fabric and add detail through stitching. Arrange the fabric leaves into the shape of their chosen bird or animal on a hessian background. When the picture is complete, sew or glue it to the background.

- Ask the children to choose one leaf and look carefully at its colour. Provide a selection of coloured papers, fabric pieces, threads, coloured pencils, crayons and paints. Ask the children to make a 'colour' sheet, on which they experiment, trying to match the colour of the leaf in a variety of media. The finished sheet might contain areas where they have tried mixing paints to achieve the colour, glued on threads and fabric or torn coloured paper from magazines.

- Show the children reproductions of paintings where famous artists have painted leaves in their pictures. *Tiger in a Tropical Storm (Surprised!)* by Henri Rousseau is a good example and gives an idea of the size of leaves in the jungle.

Cross-curricular links

SCIENCE – Show the children a flowering plant and its root system. Talk about and name the parts of the plant and their purpose. Ask the children to draw a picture of the plant, labelling the roots, stem, leaves and flower.

DESIGN AND TECHNOLOGY – Talk about the importance of fresh vegetables in our diet. Make a collection of leaves and herbs that we eat raw in salads. First check that the children do not have allergies or particular dietary requirements and then ask them to taste some of the leaves and describe their taste, texture and smell. Provide other vegetables such as tomatoes, carrots and radishes to make a colourful salad. Discuss the importance of hygiene in food preparation and safety rules when using utensils. Ask the children to work in pairs, selecting a variety of leaves and vegetables to make an attractive salad to share. Photograph the salad.

LITERACY – Look at the format of recipes in cookery books and discuss why we need recipes. Show the children a simple layout for a recipe, with the following headings:

Title:
What you need:
What to do:

Ask the children to write a recipe for the salad they have made, so that someone else could make one just like it. Add the photograph of their salad to the recipe page.

Very Fishy

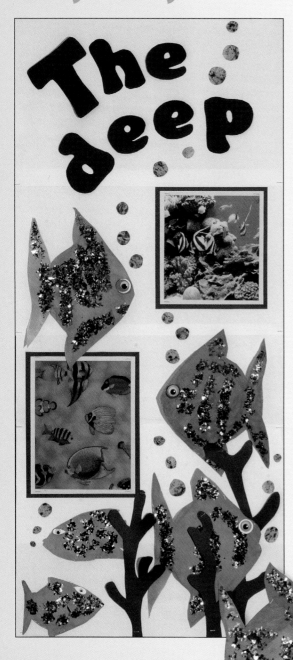

- Make a collection of pictures, books or digital resources on the theme of fish and let the children enjoy browsing through them.

- If possible, arrange for the children to see fish swimming in an aquarium and talk about the way they move and the colour and shapes of their bodies, fins and tails.

- Ask the children to notice the way in which the fish shine and shimmer in the water. Make a collection of shiny materials and objects for the children to handle and examine.

Display

1. Explain to the children that you want them to make a picture showing fish deep under water. Talk about the shapes, sizes and colours of fish, referring to books and pictures.

2. Ask the children to draw and paint fish for two separate pictures. One of these will be fish painted in 'warm' colours such as reds, oranges and yellows and one of fish painted in 'cool' colours such as blues and greens. Give the children time to experiment with mixing colours from the primary colours: red, yellow and blue.

3. Provide glitter for the children to use to add sparkle to their finished paintings. 'Googly' eyes or beads can be added for extra interest. Cut out the fish and mount the 'cool' colours on white and the 'warm' colours on blue. Cut out seaweed from green paper and air bubbles from marbled paper and add these to the display, along with pictures of other tropical fish.

Further activities

- Ask the children to look carefully at pictures of fish and make their own drawings. Enlarge the drawings onto paper and cut them out to make paper patterns. Pin the patterns onto fabric and cut out. Show the children how to apply fabric to their fishes, using simple running stitches. Provide a variety of shiny fabrics and threads to inspire the children. Mount the completed fish on another piece of fabric or sew it onto an identical piece of fabric, with the right sides together, and turn it inside out. To give a three-dimensional effect, stuff the fish with soft material.

- Let the children enjoy squeezing and rolling clay and discovering its properties. Ask them to make fish shapes by shaping the clay or using a fish-shaped cutter. To make the scales they can add small pieces of clay applied with slip. When dry, the fish can be painted and varnished.

- Provide filter paper (coffee filters are ideal) and ask the children to draw and cut out fish shapes. Brush water over the filter paper fish. The children can then drip paint onto the fish and see how the colours blend and blur on the damp paper. When dry, mount the fish on contrasting paper and hang to make mobiles.

Cross-curricular links

SCIENCE – Use sources such as books or CD ROMs to explain the life cycle of fish and how almost all fish reproduce by laying eggs. Talk about other animals which reproduce by laying eggs and ask the children to make drawings of some of these animals. Cut out the drawings and mount them to make an information sheet about life cycles.

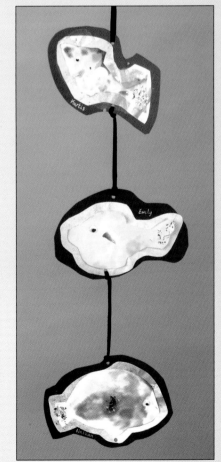

ICT – Ask the children to refer to books and pictures before drawing fish by selecting and using the pen, brush and spray tools in a computer drawing package. Show the children how to use the 'undo' command to erase a mistake. Make a slide show of the pictures or print and make them into a book to share.

DANCE – Talk about the ways in which fish move and ask the children to move like fish in different ways, for example: 'darting from side to side', 'gliding', 'turning slowly', 'swimming quickly', ''wiggling in and out of reeds', 'twisting' or 'turning round and round'.

It's Growing

Starting points

- Talk to the children about plants and trees and how they grow from seeds, developing into fully grown plants. Plant seeds such as broad beans, sunflowers or cress that the children can look after and watch grow.

- When working outdoors in soil, ensure that the area is not contaminated and is free from litter such as broken glass. Make sure that children always wash their hands after handling soil. Children should not touch seeds that have been chemically treated. When handling plants, be aware of any allergies children may have.

- In late spring or early summer, purchase bedding plants such as geraniums, petunias or fuchsias. Plant these in containers or in a patch of garden if available. Give the children the opportunity to touch, smell and examine the plants as they grow and flower, talking about their colours and texture.

Display

1. Choose a flowering plant that you want the children to use as a basis for their art work. Ask them to look carefully at the plant, noticing its colour and texture. Tell the children that you want them to make a picture of the plant and ask how they could do this.

2. Suggest that, in this instance, the children make their pictures by printing and painting. Provide a variety of objects that they can use to create the flowers. These could include cotton reels, plastic packaging, screwed-up paper or a sponge cut into petal shapes. The children should mix powder paint to a fairly thick consistency in the colour they require. Encourage the children to add leaves and a plant pot to their picture using paints and brushes.

3. When displaying the work, divide the board in half and back the two sections with contrasting papers.

Further activities

- Provide a selection of wools and strips of fabric in autumn colours for the children to use in their weaving. Prepare a strong card weaving loom approximately 30cm x 20cm. Wind wool to form the warp which runs lengthwise. Show the children how to weave wool 'over and under' to form the weft, using a large-eyed blunt needle. Explain that the following row is woven 'under and over'. They can also weave with strips of fabric using their fingers. To achieve the best effect, use a mixture of fabrics with different textures. When the weaving is completed, the children can add leaves made from fabric and artificial berries or slices of fruit.

- Find photographs, reproductions of paintings or pictures of flowers for the children to look at and talk about. Ask them to think about the colours and shapes of flowers they like and then to make a painting of a new flower that has never been seen. Cut out the finished flowers and display as 'The garden no-one has ever seen'.

- Arrange a walk in a park or garden where trees are growing. Give the children time to feel the texture of the trunks and exposed roots of the trees and to look up at them and talk about their size. Ask them to make simple line drawings of parts of a tree from differing viewpoints, such as looking up through the branches, down at the roots or viewing the tree from a distance.

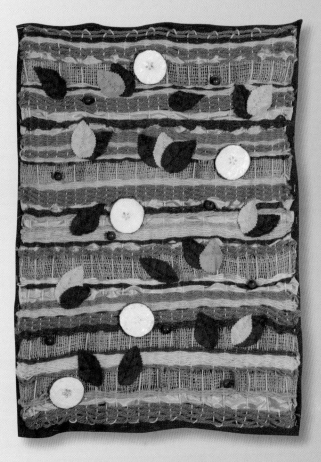

Cross-curricular links

LITERACY – When discussing how plants grow, read the children the story of 'The Gigantic Turnip'. Use the story as a starting point for role play with the children re-enacting the story. Ask the children to illustrate the story by painting and cutting out the characters to make a large wall frieze (see page 28).

PSHCE – Children's thoughtful actions can be recorded on paper leaves and added to a tree of kindness. Make a simple tree shape by cutting the trunk and branches from display paper. Cut out leaf shapes on which to record the messages. Display the tree in the hall for the whole school to share, attaching the leaves in special assemblies.

NUMERACY – Grow sunflower plants from seeds. Push a garden cane into the ground on either side of the seed. Ask the children to estimate how tall the plant will grow and mark this on one cane. Mark the weekly growth on the other cane. Encourage the children to measure themselves against the sunflower as it grows.

Living Things

Starting points

- Talk to the children about animals found in this country and their habitats. Ask them to name animals that can fly, those which live mainly on land and those which live mainly in water. List the animals they suggest under these three headings.

- Tell the children that you want them to focus on animals that could be found in or around a pond. Use sources such as books, CD ROMs, videos and the internet to show the children pictures of these animals.

- Ask the children to choose at least one animal that can fly, one that can be found in a pond and one that lives on land.

Display

1. The display will show life in and around a pond. Ask the children to paint the pond in shades of green or use fabric such as voile or net to give a three-dimensional effect. Ask the children to choose an animal that is found in the water, such as a frog. Show the children pictures of frogs and talk about their shape and colour. Ask them to paint frogs, mixing different shades of green. Cut these out and add to the display.

2. Choose together an animal that is found flying above the pond, such as a dragonfly. Paint or use collage materials for the body and bend wire or pipe cleaners to make the outline of the wings. Cover the wire with clear Cellophane or voile to make the wings. Choose an animal that is found on the land, such as a mouse or hedgehog. Paint or use fabric to make this animal and add it to the display.

3. Make plants and grasses to go around the edge of the pond by painting or using fabric. Bulrushes can be made from pieces of felt sewn together and stuffed with wadding.

Further activities

● Explain to the children that birds reproduce by laying eggs. It may be possible to observe a disused nest outside the breeding season. Ask the children to make a nest and eggs from clay. When dry, these can be painted. The children can draw a picture of the bird whose nest it is and display the picture next to the nest.

● Make a pack of cards for the children to use to play 'Snap'. Provide a set of plain cards and ask the children to look carefully at pictures of animals, choosing one animal that they would like to draw. When they have drawn and coloured the animal on one of the cards, ask them to try to make an exact copy on another card. Play 'Snap' together.

● Ask the children to think of animals that live in other countries such as lions, tigers and crocodiles. Make models of these animals using boxes and cardboard tubes. Boxes can be covered in paper or dismantled, turned inside out and reassembled to provide a plain surface on which to paint. Use buttons and pipe cleaners for the features. Either make a simple environment indoors for the models or take them outdoors into a garden area. Use the animals as a starting point for storytelling.

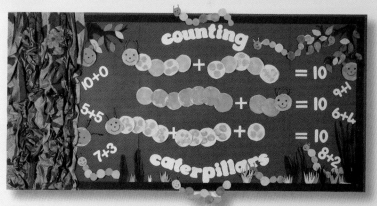

Cross-curricular links

NUMERACY – Ask the children to use plastic shapes to find different ways of making ten. Give each child ten paper circles and ask them to join them together to make two caterpillars. Count the circles that make up each caterpillar and record the results: 4 + 6 = 10; 5 + 5 = 10 and so on.

SCIENCE – Share information books about insects with the children, discussing the types of insect they may see in the local environment. Go outside on an insect hunt and make a note of where the insects were seen. Ask the children to draw and paint pictures of these insects on their return. Provide hessian, fabric scraps and sequins for the children to make pictures of insects (see page 30).

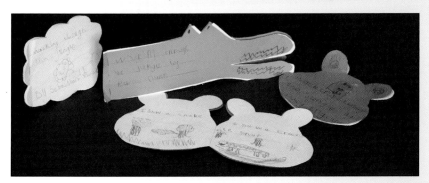

LITERACY – Read *Walking through the jungle* by Julie Lacome (Walker Books), encouraging the children to join in with the rhyming story. Use this story as a starting point for writing. Make animal-shaped booklets for the children to write about the animals they saw in the jungle. Make animal masks from card and collage materials to encourage role play.

In the Garden

- If possible, plan a visit to a park or garden so that the children can see a range of flowers and plants growing. On the way, encourage the children to talk about the different flowers they see in gardens, pots, window boxes or hanging baskets.

- In the park, take close-up digital photographs of flowers. Ask the children to look at and talk about the colours and shapes of the flowers and to find out if they are scented.

- Take paper and coloured pencils with you and ask the children to look carefully at the flowers and make drawings.

Display

1. Make up a large bunch of flowers to show the children. Give them time to enjoy the beauty of the flowers using their senses. Ask the children to look carefully at the colours. How many colours can they see? Are parts of a flower different colours or different shades of one colour?

2. Ask the children when and why we give flowers to our friends and family. Explain that you want them to make a bunch of flowers as a present for someone who helps them. This could be a member of staff or a visitor they know well.

3. Create the flowers by asking the children to draw the outline shapes on thin card using a variety of media such as oil pastels, inks, finger paints or collage materials. Add detail to the flowers with beads or buttons. Cut out the finished flowers and glue to pieces of thin dowelling. Tie the flowers in a bunch and add a gift tag.

Further activities

- Arrange to go for a walk in an area where you can see trees without leaves. Ask the children to look at the shape and size of a tree trunk and to notice how smaller branches grow from larger ones. Make a print of a tree by rolling printing ink or paint onto a board and placing torn or cut pieces of paper to make a tree shape on top of the inked surface. To take a print, lay a piece of paper on top of the board and press with a clean roller.

- Collect pictures of gardens from magazines. Ask the children to imagine that they are looking through a doorway into a secret garden. Make a wall by sponge printing paint onto paper. Mount this on polystyrene or card to give some depth to the wall and cut out the door shape. Choose and cut out a garden picture and place behind the door. Mount the finished work on a piece of card.

- Look in the garden for butterflies, or show pictures in books. Pick leaves of different sizes (ensuring that they are safe for the children to touch). Cover the leaf surfaces with paint and press onto paper to produce leaf prints. Draw butterflies on cartridge paper and colour using brightly coloured inks or paints. Cut out the butterflies and bend the wings upwards. Stick the butterfly onto the leaves, giving the effect that it has landed on the leaf.

Cross-curricular links

SCIENCE – Ask the children which animals they think live in their local environment. Visit a local park or walk around the school grounds looking for animals. For example: look under stones for woodlice, dig in soil for earthworms or observe birds visiting a bird table. Ask the children to record their findings in drawings. When working outdoors, ensure that the area is free from hazards such as broken glass and the soil is uncontaminated. Remind the children to wash their hands on their return.

PSHCE – Discuss ways to improve the school grounds by planting a container or hanging basket with flowering plants. Provide a catalogue showing bedding plants for the children to look at. Give them the opportunity to discuss and decide together the type of container, the plants and where it should be situated. When they have filled the container with flowers and put it in place, they can water and care for the plants.

DESIGN AND TECHNOLOGY – Ask the children which vegetables they think could be grown in a garden or in containers. Provide a selection of colourful salad vegetables such as radishes, cherry tomatoes, cucumber, spring onions, carrots and peppers. Ask the children to select some of the vegetables to make an attractive, healthy snack box to take on a picnic.

Colour and Light

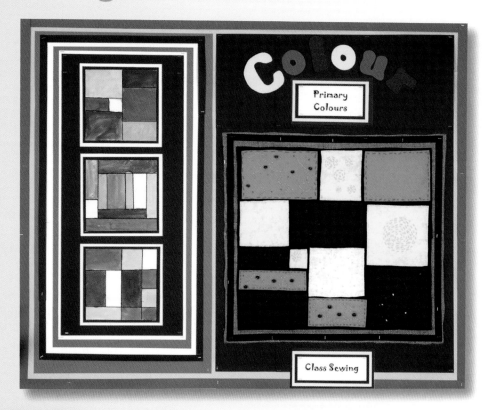

Starting points

- Set up a darkened area in the classroom or find an area in school which is dark. Ask the children to describe what they can see. Ask them if they can see shapes and colours. Gradually allow light into the space and ask again if they can see the colours of objects. Explain that, in order for us to see colour, there needs to be light.

- Ask the children to name as many colours as they can. Make a collection of objects and ask the children to sort these by colour. They will notice that there are many shades of each colour.

- Provide red, blue and yellow powder paints and explain that these are called the 'primary' colours. Ask the children to experiment by mixing two primary colours together with water and observing what happens. Aim to create greens, oranges and purples.

Display

1. Show the children examples of compositions by Piet Mondrian, where he uses rectangular blocks of colour separated by black lines. Ask the children to look carefully at these works and to paint their own pictures in a similar style.

2. Ask the children to choose one of their pictures as the basis of a design to be made in fabric. Make paper templates for each of the shapes, pin to the chosen fabric and cut out. The children can sew designs onto the pieces of fabric and embellish with buttons or beads. Glue the finished pieces to a dark background, leaving spaces between each piece.

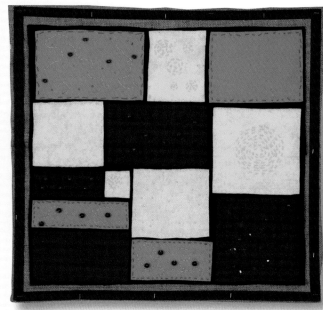

Look at our glasses.

Further activities

- Make square tiles from modelling material or clay. When the clay is dry, ask the children to paint a Mondrian-style design on their tile. The tile can be varnished when dry. If the facilities are available, the children could have their clay tiles fired in a kiln and use glazes instead of paint.

- Ask the children to make fun spectacles which enable them to see the world in different colours. They can make the spectacle frames from pieces of card and decorate them with felt-tipped pens. Pieces of Cellophane can be glued in place to form the lens.

- Discuss with the children how different colours can be linked to different moods. Ask them if they associate any particular colours with feeling happy, sad, angry or excited, giving their reasons. Provide a wide range of resources such as paints, inks, oil pastels, chalks, papers, fabric scraps and threads. Ask the children to make a 'mood picture', which illustrates through colour a feeling they have experienced. If, for example, they associate yellows and oranges with feeling happy, they would use various materials in shades of those colours.

Cross-curricular links

ICT – On the computer, ask the children to draw in the style of Piet Mondrian, using the tool for drawing rectangles and the flood fill tool. They can also experiment with changing the thickness of the lines.

LITERACY – Make a rhyming dictionary based on colour words either as a group or class project. List together as many colours as the children can name. They can then choose the words they want to include in their dictionary. Make a dictionary with pages of the appropriate colours.

SCIENCE – Talk to the children about how things look different at night when it is dark, compared to the way they look during the day. You could, for example, show them a colourful potted plant or toy against a plain background and ask them to describe it. Then show the same object in a darkened area and ask them to describe what they see. The children could record the difference by painting or drawing the object in the daylight on one half of a piece of paper and showing a night-time silhouette on the other half.

Stars

- Ask the children about the sky at night. What can they see? Where does light come from? Talk about stars; they are bodies of hot gases and appear to twinkle as their light travels through the earth's atmosphere. Explain that the sun is a star.

- Read stories and poems about stars such as *How to catch a star* by Oliver Jeffers (HarperCollins).

- Talk about the colours in the sky at night. Which colours would they use to paint a star? Which colours would they use to paint the sky at night? Ask the children to draw star shapes and choose their favourite.

Display

1. Ask one child to draw a large star shape on paper and use this as a pattern to cut out a star from a shiny fabric.

2. Spread out the star shape for the children to see and ask them to choose another piece of fabric with a different texture to make a smaller star to sew on top. Make another paper pattern for the second star and cut out the fabric. Repeat the process with a third, smaller star.

3. Provide a wide choice of sewing threads based on a gold or silver theme including wools, embroidery cottons, metallic and textured threads. Ask the children to look at the shape of their stars and sew a design suggested by the shape. They can add shiny beads, foil or sequins to embellish their designs. Stitch the completed stars in place. Wadding can be inserted behind one of the stars to give a three-dimensional effect. Mount the completed star onto a dark fabric and sew smaller stars around it, using metallic threads.

Further activities

- Make a set of starlight Christmas cards. Provide clay and two star-shaped cutters, one larger than the other. Roll the clay and cut out a star shape, and then press the smaller cutter on the top to make an indented star. Make a hole in the top of the star. When dry, the children can paint the stars and decorate with beads and glitter. Decorate a card using shiny fabric or ribbon and hang the star from the top with a tiny peg.

- Paint star shapes using different shades of yellow. Provide yellow and white powder paint and ask the children to see how many different shades of yellow they can mix to use in painting their stars.

- Talk about fireworks and their different colours and patterns. Ask the children to imagine what they would see when a new firework called 'Dizzy Stars' was lit. Use a drawing package on the computer to design the paper used as outer packaging for these fireworks. Print the designs and use to cover packets and tubes to make a box of fireworks.

Cross-curricular links

SCIENCE – Make a dark area in the classroom and provide torches for the children to experiment with light. Ask them to look for other sources of light in the classroom, such as warning lights on switches, central lights or the computer light. Talk about light sources that are used at particular times of the year such as birthday cake candles, Divali lanterns, fireworks and fairy lights.

DANCE – Ask the children to imagine that they are fireworks called 'Exploding Stars'. Discuss how they can show, through dance, the stages of the firework being lit, shooting up into the sky, exploding and dying out slowly as they fall.

MUSIC – Discuss the sounds which are made by fireworks and in particular, one called 'Whizzing Star'. Ask the children to use their voices to make a sequence of long and short sounds which depict the sounds made by the firework. One group of children could experiment with using instruments to make the firework sounds, while the rest move in response to the music.

Produced by Bushfield Fireworks Factory, Scunthorpe

All at Sea

- Talk about places the children have visited, focusing on visits to the seaside. Share resources that show pictures of people at the seaside today and in the past and discuss the things they would expect to find at the seaside.

- Make a list together. Include items such as: sand, shells, sandcastles, buckets and spades, beach huts, fish, seagulls and ice cream stalls.

- Talk about activities the children like to do at the seaside, such as: making sandcastles, paddling, playing games on the sand, listening to the sea or having a picnic.

Display

1. If possible, find an open area where the children can look at trees or houses near to them and compare these to the apparent size of similar objects in the distance. Talk about the way in which objects appear smaller the further away they are. Look at pictures that demonstrate this.

2. Look again at the seaside pictures and ask the children to describe the colours of the sea and sand on a sunny day. Talk about the way in which colours appear brighter on a sunny day. Introduce the idea of painting a seaside picture. Divide a large piece of paper into three sections and decide on the colours for the foreground, the middle ground representing the beach and the background representing the sea in the distance.

3. Ask the children to plan the picture together, showing a seaside scene. They can paint the three main sections using large brushes and then add people to the scene using smaller brushes. Remind them that the people in the distance will appear much smaller than those in the foreground.

Further activities

- Show the children pictures of brightly coloured tropical fish that are found in warm waters. Ask them to select fabrics in 'hot' colours including reds, oranges and yellows to make a collage of a tropical fish. One child can draw a simple fish shape on fabric while the other children cut out fish scales from the fabrics and sew these onto the fish with simple running stitches. To give a three-dimensional appearance, insert wadding between the scales and fish fabric. Ask the children to cut out seaweed in 'cool' colours and attach these and the completed fish to a neutral fabric.

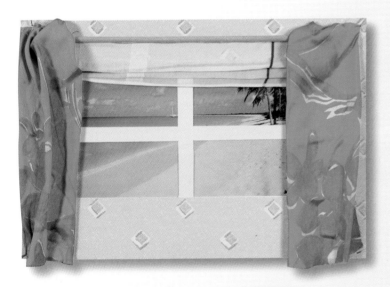

- Collect brochures of seaside holidays and ask the children to cut out some pictures of beach scenes. Talk about the colours of the sand, sea and sky. Using pieces of thin card to make a window frame, ask the children to add wallpaper, curtains and a blind made from fabric scraps and a curtain pole made from wooden dowelling. They can then place the finished window over pictures of different beach scenes and choose the view they like best.

- Ask the children to suggest which colours they associate with water. Do they think these are hot or cool colours? Prepare a shallow tray of water and ask the children to choose cool, watery colours such as blues and greens from a selection of marbling inks. Drop these onto the surface of the water and swirl the ink around with a pencil, creating patterns. Lay a piece of paper on the surface of the water to make a print of the ink patterns.

Cross-curricular links

HISTORY – Use books, digital resources or reproductions of paintings such as *Beach Scene* by Edgar Degas to show the children the types of clothes worn at the seaside in the past. Ask them to compare these with the clothes people are wearing in the holiday brochure pictures and to talk about the differences they have noticed.

GEOGRAPHY – Find the nearest seaside place on a map. Ask the children to tell you the physical features they would expect to find at the seaside. These could include a rocky area, sandy beach, cliffs, marshy area and sand dunes. Provide a variety of coloured papers and fabrics and ask the children to cut or tear these resources and use them to make a collage picture of a seaside area (see page 38).

MUSIC – Introduce the children to the idea of using musical instruments to represent different sounds. Give them time to practise making the sounds of rain falling, waves breaking, thunder and lightning. Work together using the instruments to make a sound picture, beginning with a calm sea and then showing how it starts to rain, the crescendo of a storm building up and eventually dying down again.

Whatever the Weather

Starting points

- Talk about the different kinds of weather. Ask the children to describe the weather they like best, giving reasons for their choice. Tell the children that you want them to think particularly about windy weather.

- Choose a windy day and let the children run around, feeling the wind blowing against them. Look up into the sky and see if there are clouds moving. (Remind children not to look directly at the sun, as it would be harmful to their eyes.) Can they tell where the wind is coming from? If they let go of a carrier bag or sheet of newspaper, what happens?

- Show the children a collection of kites and help them to fly them. Talk about the kite shapes and the colours used. Explain that you want them to make a big picture together, showing a windy day with lots of kites flying.

Display

1. Take a paint palette, powder paints, brushes, water and a large sheet of paper and go outside to look at the colours in the sky. Children often paint the sky a brilliant blue. Ask them if the sky is the same colour as the blue powder paint in the palette. Show the children how to add white to change the colour and how to make shades of grey. Experiment with the colours, making a variety of shades of blue and grey. Provide a large sheet of paper as the background to the picture and ask the children to paint the sky, using large brushes.

2. Ask the children which colours they would use to paint the sun. Give them time to experiment with mixing 'hot' colours such as reds, oranges and yellows and then paint the sun on the picture, using very thick paint to give a textured surface. Talk about how the weather can change quickly and a dark cloud can bring rain. Add a cloud in shades of grey and rain drops to part of the picture.

3. Ask the children to draw a large diamond shape to represent a kite and to experiment with making bright colours to paint the kite, using blocks of colour, simple shapes, stripes or dots. Cut out the kite. Add a tail made from crepe paper and staple on pieces of crepe paper to make bows along the length of the tail.

Further activities

- Provide large diamond kite shapes drawn on cartridge paper. Ask the children to mix their own hot colours to paint pictures of the sun on the kites. Cut out the kites and add tails made from coloured paper. Hang the kites at different levels from the ceiling.

- Ask the children when they would see a rainbow in the sky and which colours make up a rainbow. List these colours, red, orange, yellow, green, blue, indigo and violet. Ask the children to experiment with mixing the colours of the rainbow themselves and painting a rainbow.

- Ideally, go outside on a snowy day and make a snowman. If this is not possible, look at pictures and share stories and poems about snowmen. Tell the children that you want them to make snowmen puppets. Give each child a piece of paper approximately 10cm x 12cm and ask them to draw a snowman to fill the paper. Cut out the snowman and use as a template to make another one the same size. Glue the edges together leaving the bottom open, to make a puppet. Ask the children to use scraps of fabric and beads to make the snowman's hat, scarf, buttons and features.

Cross-curricular links

DESIGN AND TECHNOLOGY – Show the children some seaside windmills, which spin in the wind. Let them blow the windmills and see how they work. Take a windmill apart to see how it is made. Ask the children to make their own windmills by cutting out paper squares (15cm x 15cm is a good size to use). Draw diagonal lines from corner to corner and cut along these lines, almost to the centre. Fold each of the four corners to the middle and hold in place with a pin. Put a bead on the pin, at the back of the windmill and push the pin into a piece of dowelling.

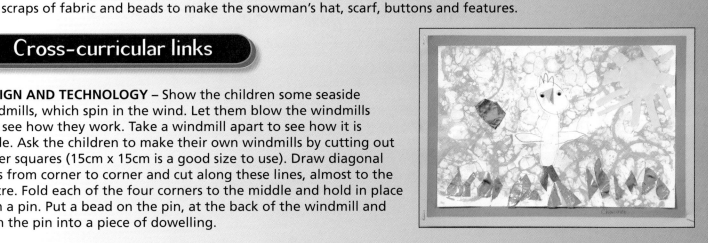

MUSIC – Sing songs related to the activities above and the weather. These could include, 'Let's go fly a kite', 'I can sing a rainbow' or 'I hear thunder'.

LITERACY – Read the story *How Billy Duck learned to swim* by Martin Waddell (Longman). Talk about Billy Duck's dislike of water and how he eventually plucked up the courage and learned to swim. Ask the children to make 'Well Done' cards for Billy Duck. Make 'bubble' paintings by blowing through a straw into diluted paint and taking a print from the bubbles. Encourage the children to draw Billy Duck and use collage materials to complete the picture.

Growing Colours

- If possible, arrange a visit to a garden centre in the summer term. Ask the children if they have ever been to a garden centre before and talk about what they expect to find there.

- During the visit, ask the children to look at the wide variety of colours of flowers and foliage. How many different colours can they see? Which colours do they like best and why? Look at the illustrations on seed packets and the huge variety of colourful flowers and vegetables that can be grown.

- Look at the different containers in which the plants are sold. Include containers of different shapes and sizes made from a variety of materials, assorted plant pots, hanging baskets or seed trays full of seedlings.

Display

1. Show the children a hanging basket or tub full of flowers. Explain that you want them to make plants to fill a hanging basket that they can hang in a role-play garden centre (see 'Further activities').

2. Ask the children to draw flowers and leaves for a hanging basket. Provide red, yellow, blue and white paint and encourage the children to experiment with mixing the paints to make a range of colours to paint the flowers. Prompt them by asking questions: How do you make purple? What will happen if you add white? How can you change green into brown?

3. Cut out the flowers and leaves. Glue or staple leaves and smaller flowers onto green string or wire to make trailing plants. Glue larger flowers and leaves onto thin garden canes. Line the hanging basket with moss or green paper and fill it with compost. Fill the basket with the flowers and leaves and hang in the role-play garden centre.

Further activities

- Create a garden centre role-play area with the children. Display real and artificial plants, the hanging basket and seedlings tray that the children have made. Add plastic plant pots, a small watering can, trowels, more artificial plants and compost. Ask the children to paint signs and pictures of plants to add to the display.

- Show the children a seed tray with small sections for growing individual plants, each filled with compost. Suggest that they make some small plants that they can use in the garden centre role-play area. Provide a collection of gardening magazines or catalogues which contain pictures of flowers. Ask the children to cut out flowers and glue them onto thin pieces of green garden cane cut into 8cm–10cm lengths. Push the flowers into the seed tray.

- Show the children how to press flowers such as busy lizzies, geraniums or buttercups between two sheets of blotting paper, with a weight on the top. Leave these for about a week and remove carefully. Provide small, oval-shaped pieces of card and ask the children to make their own miniature pictures by gluing the flowers onto the card. Display the pictures in a group.

Plants for sale

Cross-curricular links

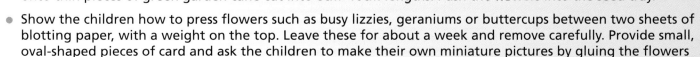

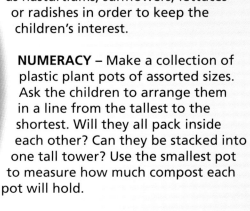

ICT – Ask the children to draw flowers using a paint program and use the flood fill tool to colour the petals. Print the pictures, cut out the flowers and use pieces of thin wire for the stems. Push the stems into a pot of compost and add the flowers to the garden centre.

SCIENCE – Use containers, or a patch of garden if available, and allow the children to plant seeds to produce their own garden colour (children should not touch chemically treated seeds). Choose quick-growing varieties such as nasturtiums, sunflowers, lettuces or radishes in order to keep the children's interest.

NUMERACY – Make a collection of plastic plant pots of assorted sizes. Ask the children to arrange them in a line from the tallest to the shortest. Will they all pack inside each other? Can they be stacked into one tall tower? Use the smallest pot to measure how much compost each pot will hold.

Ancient Egypt

Starting points

- Gather together books, pictures and resources about life in ancient Egypt. Look at pictures of ancient Egyptian writing. Talk about the hieroglyphics as picture writing and ask the children to guess the meaning of some of the pictures.

- Look at pictures of Egyptian jewellery, particularly necklaces. Ask the children to notice the colours and patterns used on the beads and the repeating patterns in the necklaces.

- Show the children stylised drawings of plants, birds and fish. Look at pictures of plants such as the papyrus flower that is depicted as a triangular shape.

Display

1. Make a vase of papyrus flowers. Make the flowers from thin card, adding patterns using oil pastels or paint. Alternatively, make them from fabric with stitched patterns. Use narrow dowelling or wire sprayed with paint for the stems. Detail can be added with sequins or beads. The children could paint stylised birds to add to the display, outlining and adding detail in black or gold.

2. Ask the children to look at pictures showing Egyptian figures and draw and paint the stylised figure of a man or woman. Again, emphasise the lines by outlining in black and use gold paint on some areas of the clothing or jewellery.

3. The children can choose books, pictures and artefacts to add to the display.

Further activities

- Suggest to the children that you work together to design an alphabet using symbols or pictures. Divide a large piece of paper into thirty rectangles (five across the top and six down the long side). Ask one child to write a the letter of the alphabet in each section using a thick marker pen and then add the symbols that the children have painted or drawn representing the letters. Use the four remaining sections to add simple pictures representing everyday words used in school, such as 'painting', 'lunch', 'book' and 'children'.

- Ask the children to make cartouches or nameplates, depicting their own names, using the symbols they have created. Note that the writing may be read from left to right, right to left or from top to bottom. The cartouche, can be made from card painted gold or silver, or from gold or silver paper glued to card. The symbols representing the letters in the child's name can be drawn or painted on paper, cut out and stuck onto the cartouche or, for a raised effect, made from modelling material and glued to the cartouche. Alternatively, make clay plaques and write and draw by pressing into the surface using a pointed clay tool. Paint the cartouches gold when dry and add to the display.

- Cut sections from paper plates to use as a basis for weaving. Make the warp threads by winding wool from the base of the flower to the outer edge. Use large-eyed blunt needles to weave different coloured wools through these threads to make the flower. Mount the flowers onto hessian, adding stems made from intertwined wool and felt leaves. Coloured beads can be sewn onto the background to complete the design.

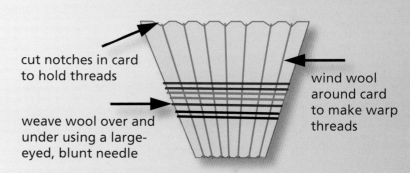

cut notches in card to hold threads

wind wool around card to make warp threads

weave wool over and under using a large-eyed, blunt needle

Papyrus

Cross-curricular links

GEOGRAPHY – Source and find information about Egypt and compare this with our own country, for example its climate, landscape and industry. Find Egypt on a map. Discuss whether it is a long way away and which forms of transport the children would use to get there from school. Show the types of transport used on their journey by using clipart images that the children have printed and cut out. Glue these onto pieces of folded card to show a sequenced, pictorial record of the journey.

ICT – Make a class or group information sheet about Egypt. Ask the children to draw pictures of themselves, adding large speech bubbles. When the children have found out facts about Egypt, they can type up the facts using the word processor, print the information, cut it out and glue it onto the speech bubbles. Cut out the completed pictures and mount these together to make an information sheet.

LITERACY – Provide the children with 'open-out' suitcases made from card (approximately 15cm x 10cm) and ask them to list inside the things they would need to take with them on a holiday to Egypt. (This provides a good opportunity to discuss sun safety and the need to take a hat and sunscreen.) Make luggage labels and ask the children to write their names in hieroglyphics. Attach the luggage labels to the suitcases.

Changing Patterns

Starting points

- Make a collection of objects such as shiny coloured stones, shells, lids from plastic bottles, bobbins, dried slices of orange, cinnamon sticks and fir cones. Display these attractively in small baskets or containers so that they are appealing to the children.

- Ask the children to use their senses when handling the objects. Encourage them to talk about the textures and say which they like to touch and why. Ask them to look for pattern in the objects and describe what they see.

Display

1. Give each child a piece of plain paper about A3 size and ask them to use any of the objects to make a pattern on the paper. Try not to lead the children or prompt them with your ideas, but allow them plenty of time to experiment and make up their own patterns. Reassure them that you want them to try out their own ideas and there is no right or wrong way to do it. Stand back and listen to their comments and photograph their work as they are doing it. Explain to the children that the photographs will be the record of their work, as the objects will be replaced in the baskets at the end of the session.

2. When they have completed their patterns, give the children the opportunity to look at and comment on everybody's work.

3. Make an interactive display to encourage other children to make their own patterns. Display the photographs of the children's finished work by attaching them to boxes of different sizes. You could use cereal or food boxes that have been covered with paper or painted. Cut out speech bubbles from card, write the children's comments inside these and glue them next to the photographs. Put the baskets of resources in front of the display to encourage other children to experiment with them. The children can rearrange the display as well as using the objects in the baskets.

Further activities

- Keep the same resources in the baskets but supply different 'bases' for the children to use as starting points for their patterns. These could include woven placemats, plastic patterned placemats, squared paper or plastic cartons.

- Vary the collection of resources by adding items such as seed heads, acorns, dried leaves, plastic clothes pegs and film cases. When the children have started making their patterns on a paper background, introduce a new resource such as thick felt-tipped pens and see how the children add to and alter their designs with their drawing.

- Introduce more reclaimed resources such as those that can be obtained from scrap stores and encourage the children to consider taking their pattern into three dimensions. For example, they could make a tower from lids, plastic tubs and pipe cleaners.

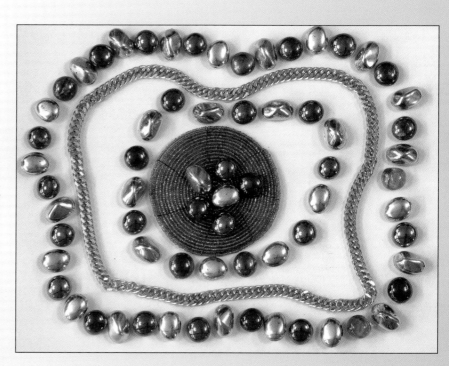

Cross-curricular links

NUMERACY – Provide the children with a selection of coloured objects, squared paper and felt-tipped pens. Ask them to use the objects to make repeating patterns in the squares such as 'blue, blue, yellow' or 'green, red, green'. When they have made the patterns they can record them on another piece of squared paper using the pens.

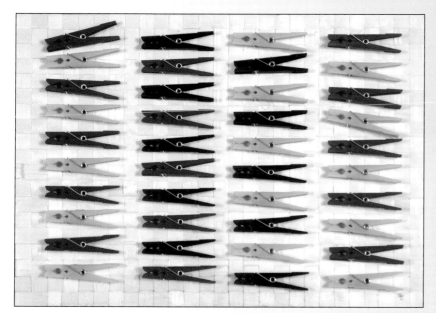

ICT – Ask the children to use a computer to make repeating patterns using stamps or clipart. Alternatively, some children could use a drawing package, draw simple shapes in a row and fill them with colour to make a repeating pattern. The children can then print out their work and add it to the display.

LITERACY – Choose some of the resources from the display and ask the children to list or tell you words that describe each object. For example, if you choose a polished stone they may say, shiny, smooth and cold. Write these words on card and laminate each one. Arrange a line of containers such as margarine tubs and put an example of the resources into each one. Put all of the words in front of the tubs and ask the children to read them and put them into the appropriate tubs.

Looking at Pattern

- Make a collection of fabrics that have clear, simple patterns. These could include fabrics with designs inspired by other cultures.

- Ask the children to look for the motifs that are repeated to make the pattern and to notice the colours used.

- Ask the children to pick out one of the motifs and use it to draw a simple pattern of their own, experimenting with drawing the motif in different positions.

Display

1. Explain to the children that you want them to print their own lengths of fabric to use in a display. Ask them to think of a motif that represents the school or area in which they live and use this as the basis of their pattern. The subjects for the motif could be as diverse as a flower, fish, block of flats or vehicle.

2. Ask the children to choose, draw and cut out a simple motif. Use this as a template to draw the motif onto polystyrene printing material. Cut out the shape and glue onto a piece of thick card to produce a printing block.

3. Use a roller to apply printing ink to the block and press firmly onto the fabric to produce a print. Repeat the process to produce a length of patterned fabric. Display the children's fabric lengths with the printing blocks next to them. Make a border for the display by printing a pattern onto strips of paper.

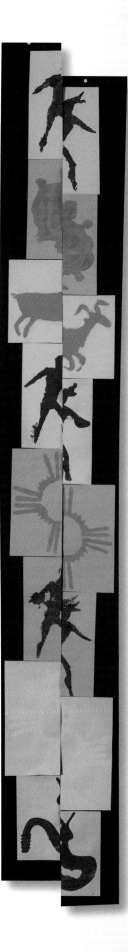

Further activities

- Choose a theme such as 'sunburst' or 'animals' and ask the children to draw an appropriate shape. Use this to make a printing block as on the previous page. Provide strips of paper and ask the children to print their patterns along the length of the paper. When dry, the children can cut or tear the strip vertically through the centre of the pattern and mount both halves on a piece of coloured paper, with one piece slightly higher than the other to produce a new 'broken' pattern.

- Use a theme that fits in with other areas of the curriculum and ask the children to choose and draw simple shapes linked to that theme. Cut out the shapes, for example animals, and draw around them on a square of card to produce a pattern. 'Paint' the shapes with glue and sprinkle coloured sand over them. Shake to remove the excess sand. Repeat using different-coloured sand.

- Ask the children to create a pattern based on mathematical shapes such as circle, square and triangle, drawn on a square of thin paper using fabric crayons. The completed pattern can then be transferred onto a piece of fabric, following the manufacturer's instructions.

Cross-curricular links

SCIENCE – When talking about life cycles, record these in simple patterns on strips of paper, showing how the cycle is repeated. For example, this could be a bird, egg, chick, which are then repeated, or a seed, seedling, flower and seed head.

DESIGN AND TECHNOLOGY – Ask the children to work together to design and make a display for another area of the curriculum, for example a geography display about the seaside. Included in the display will be a length of fabric that they have designed. Talk about things the children associate with the seaside, such as buckets and spades, ice creams, fish or sandcastles. Ask them to draw motifs to make repeating patterns on a piece of fabric using fabric markers. The children can collect artefacts, books and pictures to include in their display.

MUSIC – Ask the children each to choose a percussion instrument and to work with a partner making musical patterns. They could, for example, shake a tambourine twice and then tap a wood block three times and repeat this pattern several times. More confident children can make more complicated patterns or use more instruments.

Patchwork Patterns

Starting points

- Make a collection of items with simple, decorative patterns such as fabrics, wrapping paper or gift bags. Give the children the opportunity to handle these, saying which they like and why.

- Provide coloured bricks, blocks or cubes and ask the children to make a pattern using these. Take photographs showing their different designs.

- Give each child a piece of squared paper (the younger the children, the larger the squares) and ask them to paint a pattern using the squares.

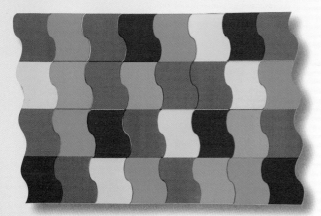

Display

1. As part of numeracy work, introduce the song 'Ten in the bed', to help the children understand the concept of subtraction. Sing the song together with ten children sitting in a row on the floor with a cover over them. As they all roll over and one falls out, the children see that there is now one less child in the bed.

2. Suggest to the children that they make a big picture to illustrate the song and to help them count and recognise the numbers one to ten. Ask them to choose, paint and cut out ten toys to go in the bed. Paint and cut out the numbers one to ten. Pin the pictures and numbers together on the wall.

3. Ask the children what is missing and what the toys need in order to keep them warm in bed. If possible, show them a patchwork quilt and suggest that they paint a patchwork quilt for the toys' bed, using the ideas they had when making patterns with bricks and cubes or when painting on squared paper. Divide a large piece of paper into squares and ask the children to mix colours and paint their own patchwork quilt.

Further activities

- Provide a selection of textured papers, bubble wrap, corrugated card and small pieces of coloured plastic bags for the children to explore and describe. Ask them to make a textured patchwork by cutting the materials into squares, rectangles or other regular shapes and gluing them close together on backing paper.

- Ask the children to roll out salt dough and cut out circles using a biscuit cutter. Dry out the circles in an oven on a low heat. When cold, paint the circles. Suggest that the children use the circles to make a three-dimensional patchwork pattern on a piece of thick cardboard and glue them in place.

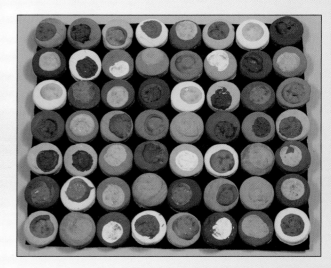

- Provide a length of plain fabric, pots of printing inks or paints and pieces of sponge cut into squares. Ask the children to print a patchwork pattern on the fabric using the sponge squares to make a cover to use when they sing 'Ten in the bed'.

Cross-curricular links

ICT – Use a simple drawing program and ask the children to design a patchwork quilt using the shape and flood fill tools. You could limit their use of colours to 'warm' or 'cool' colours.

RELIGIOUS EDUCATION – At harvest time, make a collection of fruits or vegetables and use these to make a harvest patchwork. Place a cloth on a table or use a shallow box and ask the children to make a pattern from the fruits and vegetables by placing them close together to make a colourful and edible patchwork.

PSHCE – During circle time, talk about working towards simple goals. Ask the children to think of one thing they cannot yet do but would like to achieve. This might include goals such as being able to catch a ball, skip, swim five

metres, thread a needle or keep their bedroom tidy. Give each child a piece of coloured paper approximately 10cm square on which to write their name and their goal. Glue the squares onto backing paper to make a pattern quilt. Use the quilt as a talking point to raise self esteem as the children achieve their goals.

Machines

Starting points

- Ask the children to think about machines that they have in their homes, such as washing machines, tumble driers, dishwashers, lawn mowers, sewing machines or bicycles. Ask them to tell you about the parts of the machines that move, how they move and the jobs they do.

- Let the children use their bodies to show the ways the moving parts of machines can work. They could show turning movements with their hands, up-and-down movements by stamping their feet and side-to-side movements by moving their bodies from left to right.

- Collect pictures of machines and ask the children to identify the three-dimensional shapes they can see that have been used in making the machines. These could include cubes, cuboids, cylinders and cones.

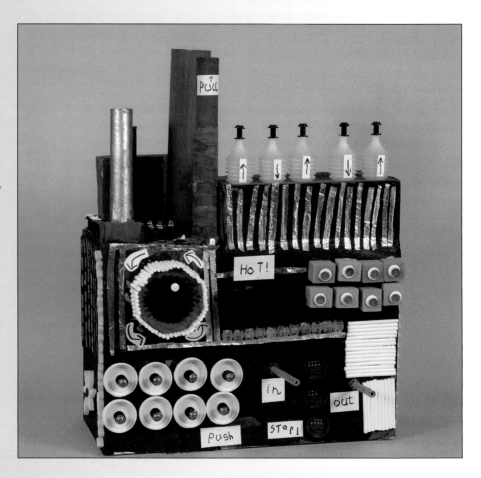

Display

1. Explain to the children that they are going to make a machine with moving parts. Provide a collection of boxes of differing shapes and sizes and ask them to experiment with arranging them in a shape which will be the basis of their machine. (If you dismantle any printed boxes and reassemble them inside out, you will have a good surface on which to paint.) Glue or tape the boxes together.

2. Make a collection of toys with moving parts and use these to give the children ideas about how to make moving parts for their machine. They can attach lids or circles of card with a split pin in the centre and a cork added as a handle. Cut holes in the boxes and push pieces of cane or dowelling backwards and forwards or attach a rectangle of card by one side so that it can be opened like a door. A cardboard tube threaded onto a piece of dowelling can be turned round and round.

3. When the machine is completed it can be painted. Try limiting the colours the children use, for example asking them to use only black, white, silver and grey.

Further activities

- Ask the children to draw and cut out card circles of different sizes and then paint a design that radiates from the centre like the spokes of a bicycle wheel. Add a 'handle' made from a paper fastener to each circle. Push paper fasteners through the centre of each circle and attach them to a piece of card. The children can turn the wheels around and experience the colour effects.

- Choose a favourite story such as *Owl Babies* by Martin Waddell (Walker Books) or a traditional story or rhyme that the children would like to illustrate. Choose one scene from the story and ask the children to represent it on a piece of card, using a mixture of their own drawings and clipart images that they have printed and cut out. Ask them to choose one illustration which will have a moving part. This could be an owl's wing moving up and down (attach a wing with a paper fastener) or Red Riding Hood moving through the forest (help the children make a simple slider and attach a cut-out figure to this).

- Show the children a bicycle and ask them to look closely at the parts that move, for example the cogs and chain, brakes or pedals. Let them take close-up photographs of these parts using a digital camera. Print the photographs and assemble to make one collage picture.

Cross-curricular links

SCIENCE – Talk to the children about how they can make things move. Ask them to look around the classroom and find things that need pushing or pulling to make them move. These could include light switches, the ON/OFF switch on a computer, a drawer, a door or a toy vehicle. Challenge the children to make a toy car move without pushing or pulling it.

DANCE – Ask the children to imagine that they are machines that have been switched off. They must stand very still. Then ask them to imagine that the machine is now switched on and they can experiment with moving parts of their bodies using a repetitive movement, such as clapping their hands, stamping their feet or punching the air. On your signal the machines stop working or start again.

NUMERACY – Give the children time to handle, name, describe and build machines with a wide variety of solid shapes. Encourage them to describe the shapes using words such as, flat, curved, side, face, corner, solid and hollow.

Triangles

- Go on a triangle hunt around school. Take photographs to use for reference later and make a collection of triangles for the children to sort by size, shape or colour.

- Give the children opportunities to understand the properties of triangles by asking them to hold hands and make a large triangle. Encourage them to move and make triangles of different shapes. They can use skipping ropes, benches or other P.E. equipment to make triangles on the floor and use these as part of a P.E. lesson, for example by walking around the edges or jumping in and out of the shapes.

- Use chalk to draw large shapes, including triangles, on the playground. The children run around and, when you call 'triangle sides', 'triangle corners' or 'inside a triangle', they run and stand in the appropriate place.

Display

1. Photocopy a page of equilateral triangles that are all the same size. Ask the children to cut these out and experiment with making patterns by fitting the triangles together.

2. Explain to the children that they are going to develop these pattern ideas by making and decorating their own triangles in fabric rather than paper, then fitting the triangles together to create one large design.

3. Provide each child with an equilateral triangle of plain fabric which will not fray, such as felt, with sides of approximately 15cm. These could be cut from random colours, shades of one colour or limited to two or three colours. Provide a wide variety of threads, string and wools for the children to sew designs onto the triangles. They can add buttons or sequins by gluing these to the fabric. When completed, ask the children to experiment with arranging the triangles on a backing to create a new shape; this example shows the triangles arranged to form a fish image. Display the created image on a suitable background, adding detail such as seaweed and other sea creatures.

Further activities

- Give the children an opportunity to experiment with printing and overprinting onto paper or fabric using triangles as the theme. Triangles could be cut from sponges, potatoes, card or polystyrene printing material designed for use in schools. Look at the effect when one colour is printed over another.

- Using the computer, ask the children to use the straight-line tool to create lines that criss-cross over the page. Ask them to use the flood fill tool to colour all of the triangles they have made.

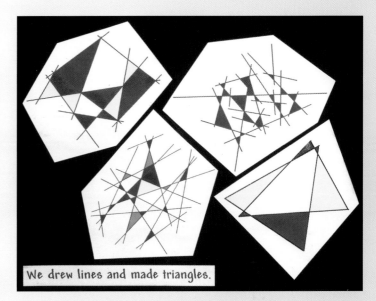

We drew lines and made triangles.

- Cut cartridge paper into equilateral triangles of the same size. Ask the children to choose one colour and start by painting a line along one side of the triangle. They can then add a small amount of white paint to the colour they have chosen and paint another line close to it. Repeat this process until the triangle is covered. Encourage the children to talk about the effect they have achieved and how the colour changed as they added more white. Use the finished triangles to create different designs.

Cross-curricular links

MUSIC – Provide triangles and give the children time to experiment with playing them. Ask the children to make simple repeating patterns when striking the triangles, such as '123 pause, 123 pause, 123' or making sounds which get louder and then softer. Experiment with ways of recording their musical patterns, by drawing triangles. For example:

1   2   3   pause   1   2   3   pause   1   2   3   (sounds getting louder and then softer)

DESIGN AND TECHNOLOGY – Design and make pizzas to take on a 'shape' picnic. Provide dough for the pizza bases and a variety of toppings such as sliced cheese, tomatoes and courgettes. Ask the children to make rectangular pizzas and, when cooked, cut the pizzas into smaller rectangles, squares and triangles of different sizes.

NUMERACY – Ask the children to make triangles using coloured elastic bands on a pinboard. Encourage them to count the number of triangles they have made, noticing if they have created more triangles where triangles overlap.

Buildings

In the city

- Take the children into the environment around the school and ask them to look at the different shapes they see in the buildings around them. Look at the shapes used in tiles, brickwork, wooden panels in doors, fences, stonework, roofs, windows and paving.

- Take digital photographs and display these, using them as a record of what they have seen and as starting points for discussion.

- Ask the children to describe the shapes they have noticed on their walk and which shape seems to be used most in buildings.

Display

1. Show the children pictures of different types of built environment, including recently constructed buildings, older buildings and industrial landscapes. Look at the skylines together and talk about the different shapes they notice. Go into the local area and ask the children to make simple drawings of buildings, showing the skyline.

2. Talk about the shapes, patterns and textures they have noticed on walls, doors and windows, referring to the photographs they have taken. Ask the children to choose either one of their drawings or a picture of a built environment, to use as the starting point for their display.

3. Go for a walk and ask the children to feel the textures they see in bricks, stone and wood (checking first that it is safe to do so). Take rubbings of these textured surfaces by covering the surface with paper and rubbing a wax crayon over it. Examine the collection of rubbings and talk about the different patterns and textures they have created. Ask the children to cut these pieces of paper into the shapes of buildings to use in their display. Paint a large background to represent the sky and glue or staple the building shapes in place.

Further activities

- Ask the children to draw a house by pressing into a piece of polystyrene printing material with a pencil or ball-point pen. Ensure they include detail such as doors and windows. Cut out the house shape. Roll printing ink over the block and press the inked side firmly onto paper. Make several prints before washing the block. When the prints are dry, make some changes to the block, for example you could cut off the roof and draw some bricks on the wall. Use a different-coloured ink to cover the block and press the inked side on top of the first print.

- Look at the pattern created when bricks are laid to make a wall. Ask the children to feel the texture of the bricks. Provide clay and ask each child to make a brick-shaped tile approximately 1cm–1.5cm thick and experiment with making different surface textures. They could brush the surface with a stiff brush, drag a comb across it, roll a fir cone over it or press objects into it. When the tiles are dry the children could assemble all of the tiles on a strong backing board to make their own wall.

- Ask the children if they think circles and curved shapes are often used when building walls of houses. Provide salt dough or clay and ask them to work with a partner, rolling long 'sausages' of dough to build walls as they experiment with making a model of a circular house. When the walls are in place, ask the children to work out how they can make a roof from card.

Cross-curricular links

ICT – Look at pictures of a cityscape at night, showing the windows lit up against a dark building. Ask the children to use the rectangle and flood fill tools on a computer to draw a cityscape at night. Remind them how to use the 'undo' command if they make a mistake or want to change something.

NUMERACY – Talk about the fact that buildings are made from shapes that fit together. Provide a collection of triangles, rectangles, circles and squares, ensuring all of the shapes of one kind are the same size. Ask the children to work with a partner and see which shapes will fit together without leaving any spaces (tessellate). Ask them to photograph their patterns and report their findings to the rest of the group.

DESIGN AND TECHNOLOGY – Go for a walk in the local area, looking at doors and doorways. Ask the children to find as many different styles and shapes as possible. Take photographs and ask the children to make drawings as a record of what they have seen. Refer to these and ask the children to work with a partner to make a three-dimensional door and doorway using a cardboard box. Discuss ways in which they can make hinges to attach the door to its surround. Discuss together which hinges were the most successful and why. Experiment in achieving different effects to represent the materials used in the door and surrounding wall.

Looking for Shapes

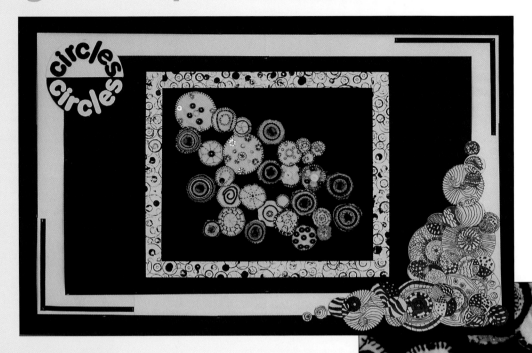

Starting points

- Make a collection of old and new toys, including some with wheels. Ask the children to examine the toys carefully, looking for shapes they know, such as circles, rectangles and triangles.

- Ask the children to count how many circles they can see, also looking for circles inside circles. Take close-up photographs of the circles they have found and use these to stimulate discussion.

- Provide a range of plastic mathematical shapes and ask the children to sort all of the circles into one pile. Give them time to explore the properties of the circles, for example, comparing the sizes, stacking them according to size, rolling them or making patterns with them.

Display

1. Choose two contrasting colours for the display, such as black and white. The fabric you use as a base for the sewing activity should be fairly substantial, such as a linen type. Cut circles from contrasting fabrics and sew designs onto them using a variety of threads in the same colour as the backing fabric. To give texture and depth to their work, the children could incorporate large metal washers, buttons, curtain rings or circles made from scrunched cooking foil into their sewing. Attach these sewn circles to the printed backing by stitching or gluing.

2. Make a collection of circular objects of varying sizes to use for printing. These could include large card circles, ends of tubes, bases of plastic bottles or wheels from construction kits. Ask the children to print a border of circles for the display, using these objects. Print the circles close together, overlapping or with smaller circles printed inside larger ones. Mount the display on this printed border.

3. Using circle templates, create an overlapping circle design to use as a corner border for the display. The children can infill the design with patterns for impact.

Further activities

- Make small, circular card looms. Ask the children to choose three colours of wool for their weaving and to use one of these to make the warp threads. To do this, wind the wool through the central hole and over the edges of the card. The children can then weave through these threads using a large-eyed, blunt needle.

- Provide a commercially produced polystyrene printing material cut into squares. Ask the children to draw a design based on two-dimensional shapes, by pressing into the surface of the foam with a pencil or ballpoint pen. Squeeze printing inks onto boards and ask the children to use a roller to apply the inks they have chosen to their printing blocks. Press the inked side down firmly onto a piece of fabric, producing a pattern by fitting the shapes together.

- Collect a variety of different-sized cardboard tubes. Ask the children what shape they can see at the ends of each tube. Ask them to experiment in making a three-dimensional design using the cylinders. They can cut the tubes into different lengths and place them next to or inside each other. The tubes can be glued together on a card base to make a new structure which can be painted or sprayed.

Cross-curricular links

NUMERACY – Make up a simple shape game to help children identify two-dimensional shapes. Ask the children to help to make two sets of cards. On one set they write questions such as: 'I have 4 corners, 2 short sides and 2 long sides. What am I?' On the other set they draw the appropriate shape.
Children take it in turns to read the questions and find the correct matching shape.

DESIGN AND TECHNOLOGY – Provide a collection of outdoor play toys such as prams, tractors, wheelbarrows and cars. Talk about the features of the vehicles and why wheels are circular. Ask the children to observe and discuss the number and sizes of the wheels and the different shapes of the vehicles. Show the children how the wheels are attached to the axles and give them the opportunity to experiment with attaching wheels to axles using construction kits or wooden wheels with dowelling axles.

SCIENCE – Ask the children to look at the collection of outdoor play vehicles and challenge them to work out how to make the vehicles move. Let them experiment with pushing or pulling the vehicles and talk about what they have found out. Provide a collection of small vehicles and ask the children if they can work out ways to move any of these without pushing or pulling them. They may suggest that they can let them roll down a slope or blow them along.

Jack-in-a-box

Starting points

- Read the story *Just like Jasper!* by Nick Butterworth and Mick Inkpen (Hodder Children's Books).

- Make a collection of toys, some of which use the 'Jack-in-a-box' principle. Give the children time to enjoy playing with the toys and to speculate about how they work.

- Collect a variety of large cardboard boxes and ask the children to sort them into cubes and cuboids. Let the children experiment with being a real-life Jack-in-a-box by crouching down inside one of the boxes and springing up when a child taps on the box.

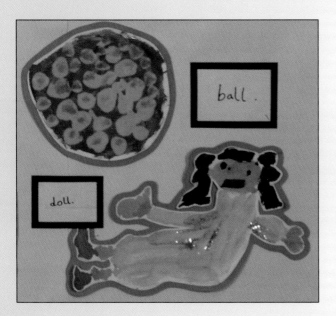

Display

1. Explain to the children that you want them to make a big picture showing Jasper jumping up like a Jack-in-a-box. Ask a group of children to refer to the illustrations in the book and draw, paint and cut out a large picture of Jasper. Staple the picture to the wall, inserting loosely scrunched paper behind it to give a three-dimensional effect.

2. Cover a large box with paper and decorate the sides. Fill the box with coloured paper and attach to the wall, below Jasper. Add party streamers and balloons.

3. Ask another group of children to draw and paint the toys which Jasper saw in the toyshop. Cut these out and add to the display. Add labels and speech bubbles.

Further activities

- Ask the children to consider how they could make a model containing something which jumps out of a box when the lid is opened. One way is to coil a large pipe cleaner into a spiral to make a spring. Construct boxes by making cubes from nets, leaving one part open for the lid. Decorate the boxes. Ask the children to draw and cut out card figures which will pop out of the box. Attach the figure to the top of the pipe-cleaner spring and attach the bottom of the spring to the base of the box. Close the lid. When the lid is opened, the figure will pop up.

- Look at examples or pictures of wooden toys from the past. Show the children some wooden spoons and traditional wooden 'dolly' pegs and suggest that they make peg or spoon dolls. Use a felt-tipped pen or paint to draw in the facial features, adding purchased 'googly' eyes and wool for the hair. Wrap a pipe cleaner around the spoon to make the arms and use a square of fabric or crepe paper to make a dress, cutting small holes for the neck and arms.

- Ask the children to bring small toys from home and display these as exhibits in a museum. Lay shoe boxes on their sides and tape or glue them together to make a display unit. The children can paint the insides of the boxes and display one toy in each box. Ask them to make labels for each item.

Cross-curricular links

NUMERACY – Make a collection of cubes. These could be boxes, tins or bricks. Ask the children to examine a cube and discover its properties. How many faces does it have? What shape are the faces? How many edges? How many corners? Is it solid or hollow?

HISTORY – Ask the children to bring a favourite toy to show the rest of the class. Borrow old toys from a museum service or use pictures and ask a grandparent to come and talk to the children about their toys. Compare old and new toys of a similar type, such as bears or vehicles. Ask the children to tell you how the toys are similar and how they are different.

DANCE – Ask the children to move like toys such as a Jack-in-a-box. They can curl up small as if they are in the box and, on a signal, jump up high with their hands in the air. When the 'lid' is replaced they are squashed down again into the box. Also experiment with moving like other toys such as a toy soldier, a remote-controlled car or a bouncing ball.

What is Inside?

Starting points

- Make a collection of objects that can have something placed inside them which cannot be seen, such as a box, tin, doll's house, shoe bag, lunch box or teapot. Place an unexpected object inside each item, for example an egg in a teapot, a toy frog in a lunch box or some flowers in a shoe bag.

- Present the collection to the children and let them have fun guessing what might be inside. Talk about how we wrap presents to hide the contents and surprise the recipient. Hide a present inside a box for the children. Let them speculate about what might be inside. When the children open the box, it could reveal a plate containing a smiling face made from pieces of fruit for their snack.

- Find examples of packing that is used to separate and protect the contents, such as a tray inside a box of chocolates, egg boxes or the indented polystyrene used in boxes of apples. Ask the children to arrange small objects such as beads, stones, fir cones or recycled items inside the sections of the packing material.

Who is hiding?

Peep inside.

Display

1. Talk to the children about the animals that they might find living in a tree, such as squirrels, birds, insects or spiders. Explain that you want them to make a 'Tree of surprises', with animals hidden inside the trunk. Collect cardboard boxes of differing sizes. Boxes can be dismantled and reassembled inside out, providing a plain surface on which to paint or collage. Glue and tape the boxes together to make a structure for the tree trunk. Cut doors of different shapes and sizes into the boxes, leaving one side attached to make a hinge. Make handles for the doors from items such as large wooden beads, a length of paper clips fixed together, clothes pegs attached to the side of the door or a pipe cleaner pushed through a hole and knotted on the inside.

2. Discuss together how to make the surface of the boxes look like a tree trunk. Mix powder paints in shades of browns and greens and sponge print onto the trunk. Make the branches from paper and print in the same way as the trunk. Attach the branches to a display board above the trunk.

3. Ask the children to choose animals they want to make to hide in the tree. Remind them that it is a tree of surprises and ask them to include one animal that would be completely unexpected, such as a crocodile or fish. Use modelling material such as dough or clay to make the animals. Hide the animals inside the boxes.

Further activities

- Look at other ways of putting something inside something else. Show the children how objects can be enclosed inside two layers of book-covering film or a laminating pouch. Provide a collection of items such as coloured tissue paper, string, wool, glitter and sequins. Ask the children to make their own designs on the sticky side of the book-covering film or the inside of the laminating pouch with the materials provided. If using book-covering film, lay another piece of film on top of the finished design to enclose it. If using a laminating pouch, laminate to secure the design inside. Thread several designs together to create a mobile.

- Ask the children to look at the colours of leaves and experiment with mixing those colours using the primary colours, red, yellow and blue. Ask them to paint the outline of a leaf shape onto a piece of A3-sized paper, using a thick brush. Then paint another leaf-shaped outline inside using another colour. Continue painting leaf shapes inside the leaf until there is no space left. Talk about the colours they have made by mixing primary colours together.

- Make a collection of non-fiction books showing pictures of animals the children have made for the tree. Ask them to refer to the pictures and draw the animals on thick card (approximately 10–15cm high) in order to make stick puppets. Provide collage materials such as fabrics, pipe cleaners and a variety of threads for the children to use to create the animals. Tape a stick behind the finished puppets and use these in role play.

Cross-curricular links

SCIENCE – Ask the children to think about natural objects that are found inside something else. These could include: a horse chestnut inside its shell; orange segments inside the skin; a snail inside its shell; a baby mammal inside its mother; seeds inside a pomegranate. Talk about the reasons why some things are inside others. Make a collection of fruits that have seeds inside them and cut these open. Examine and compare the sizes of the seeds.

NUMERACY – Use the animals from the 'Tree of surprises' as a starting point for developing the language of position and size. Ask the children to place the animals somewhere in relation to the tree. For example, 'Put the mouse next to the smallest door/behind the largest door/next to the tree/in front of the tree'.

LITERACY – Encourage the children to use the animal puppets they have made as starting points for role-play activities. Ask them to sit on the floor behind a table and hold the puppets above the table top to give an impromptu performance for their friends.

Flashing Eyes

Starting points

- Share stories and poems about dragons, such as *Dragon Poems* by John Foster and Korky Paul (Oxford University Press).

- Ask the children to describe a dragon, imagining what its skin would feel like, the colour of its eyes, skin, the inside of its mouth and the fire it breathes. Tell the children that you want them to make their own dragons.

- Ask the children how you could make a dragon's eyes come to life so that they would actually flash. Explain that you could use a simple circuit to give the dragon flashing eyes.

Display

1. Ask the children to draw a dragon approximately 30cm long on stiff card. Discuss and choose a way to give the skin texture. The children will have their own ideas, but they could apply very thick paint with a knife (using powder paint mixed with PVA glue) or they could glue crumpled fabric to the surface and then paint it. Sponge print a piece of card to use as a background and glue the dragon to this.

2. Insert a bulb for the eye and complete the circuit at the back of the piece of card (see 'Cross-curricular links'). Ask the children to decide how to show the fire coming from the dragon's mouth. They could use brightly coloured plastic laces, torn tissue paper or painted twigs. Invite the children to choose what they want to use in the foreground of their picture and add objects such as rocks, stones or coloured sand. They could add a thought bubble to the dragon.

Further activities

- Ask the children to press or roll clay into a plaque or tile shape and then draw a dragon in the clay using a clay tool. Ask them to think about the texture of the skin and press objects into the clay to give a textured finish. When dry, paint and varnish the tile.

- Talk about the skin texture of different animals and ask the children to experiment by using different substances to create different effects. They could mix paint and PVA glue together and add substances such as sawdust or sand, or paint on textured surfaces such as corrugated card, bubble wrap, sandpaper or bark.

- Provide the children with small cardboard boxes, card, pens, scissors and glue and challenge them to use their knowledge of making circuits to make a picture or object that will light up. If children need ideas to help them get started, suggest drawing a face with a nose that lights up or a lighthouse with a light on the top.

Cross-curricular links

LITERACY – Ask the children to work with a partner and make up a story about a dragon. Ask questions such as: Where does the dragon live? Where has it been? What is it doing? How is it feeling? Where is it going? Is it alone? What happens next? Ask the children to plan the outline of their story. Make a page for them to use for their story writing by folding a piece of A4 paper into four and cutting out a dragon's bite-sized piece from one corner. The children can use the outer page as a cover and write their story on the inside pages.

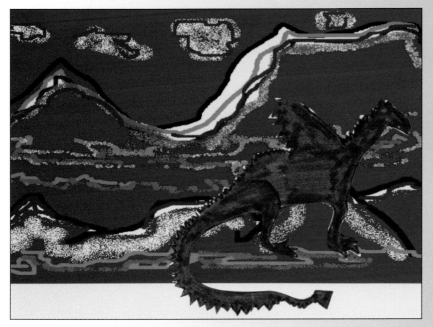

SCIENCE – Give the children batteries, insulated wires and bulbs and ask them to work out how to make a bulb light up. When they have completed this task, challenge them to make their dragon's eye light up. Ask them to make drawings showing their working circuits and explain why they work.

ICT – Ask the children to use a simple computer paint package to create a fantasy scene where the dragon might live, using clipart to add detail. Ask them to print out their work and talk about why they used particular pictures.

Disguise a floor turtle as a dragon. Put the dragon's eggs at a distance from the dragon and ask the children to program the dragon to be able to find its way back to its eggs.

Flowers

- Arrange a walk in a park or garden in spring or summer and give the children time to enjoy looking at the flowering plants and trees. Walking under cherry trees in bloom on a windy day provides a wonderful experience as the children will be showered with petals.

- Ask the children to notice and describe the colours of the tree trunks and the flower petals. Take photographs with a digital camera and use these for reference later.

- Collect fallen petals and a small flowering branch to use as a starting point for the children's observational drawings.

Display

1. Ask the children to look carefully at the collected branch or plant, noticing its lines, shapes and colours. They can look at it and photograph it from different angles, including from above.

2. Give the children time to experiment with mixing powder paints to recreate the colours of the branch or plant. This provides a good opportunity to encourage discussion about colours and develop language associated with colour such as, 'different shades of', 'darker', 'lighter', 'pale', 'warm colours' and 'cool colours'.

3. After their observations and experiments with mixing the colours, ask the children to paint a pale blue background on which to create their picture. They should choose a viewpoint and paint a picture of the flowering plant or branch, trying to paint the same lines and colours they observe. Mount the images onto a dark background and add cut-out flowers for impact.

Further activities

- Collect plants such as primulas, which can be found in several different colours. Show the children how to press a selection of the flower heads between pieces of paper, placing a weight on the top. Ask them to paint leaves and cut these out using scissors which give a serrated finish. Print flower shapes in the centre of the leaves, using found objects such as small plastic cogs, dipped into paint. The centres of the flowers can be printed using the end of a piece of dowelling. Complete the picture by adding the pressed flowers and simple leaves made from felt.

- Arrange a walk in a park or garden to look at flowers, or provide a collection of large flowers in bold colours for the children to examine. Show the children how to mix powder paint to a thick consistency. Ask them to paint pictures of the flower heads, applying the paint with a piece of card to achieve a textured finish.

- Collect flowers with 'sun's ray' petals, such as daisies, chrysanthemums or sunflowers. Place a blob of ink on a piece of paper and ask the children to blow through a straw onto the ink, sending it outwards into spiky petal shapes, to create the 'flower heads'.

Cross-curricular links

PSHCE – When walking in the school grounds or local area, ask the children particularly to notice any planted areas or gardens. Ask them to think about how plants and trees improve their environment. Encourage the children to discuss the importance of caring for their environment so that it is attractive for everyone to enjoy. Plant a container with seasonal flowers to improve the area outside the classroom.

SCIENCE – Talk about the fact that fruits contain seeds and these are produced from flowers. Make a collection of fruits such as tomato, apple, pepper, mango and avocado. Cut these in half and ask the children to find and compare the seeds, talking about their size, colour and shape.

NUMERACY – Look at flowering plants in a garden or in containers. Talk about the sizes of the plants and encourage the use of language related to size and position, for example, 'taller', 'tallest', 'shorter', 'shortest', 'next to', 'in front of' or 'behind'. Make a picture showing plants of differing sizes, to use as a talking point.

Colour Design

- Make a collection of objects with designs based on stripes, such as gift bags, wrapping paper, mugs, plates or fabric. Look also at reproductions of the paintings of Bridget Riley.

- Ask the children to look carefully at the use of colour. Are the designs based on one colour, using contrasting colours or many colours? Talk about the designs used and which the children prefer and why.

- Choose one of the designs and show the children how they can make a similar design but make it look very different by using different colours. Give the children the opportunity to experiment using thick felt-tipped pens to try out their ideas.

Display

1. Tell the children that you want them to experiment with mixing colours using powder paints and to apply the paint in stripes on squares of paper. The children can use oil pastels to add more stripes or emphasise those they have painted.

2. Explain that, if each child draws their design on one small square, they can then arrange all of the squares together to make one large design.

3. The completed designs can be arranged on a large sheet of paper or glued onto the sides of boxes to make a three-dimensional display.

68

Further activities

- Provide a selection of drawing inks, brushes and small squares of paper. Let the children experiment with drawing lines with the inks, noticing the different effects they can achieve. Ask the children to look at new shapes created where the inks have run and emphasise these shapes by drawing around them with oil pastels. Mount the squares close together to make a large design.

- Collect brightly coloured collage materials that can be used to

make stripes, such as coloured papers, Cellophane, plastic, yarns and fabrics. These could be a random mix of colours or colours on a theme, such as 'Christmas', 'Autumn' or 'Sunshine'. Ask the children to cut these materials into strips and place them close together to make a striped design. Glue the pieces in place.

- Choose a theme that fits in with another area of the curriculum, for example the seaside, and ask the children to make a clay picture depicting an appropriate scene. Ask them to tell you which colours they associate with the seaside and to choose just four or five colours to use when painting their clay picture.

Cross-curricular links

ICT – Using a simple drawing program on the computer, create a design for wrapping paper, based on a simple shape such as a circle or square. Ask the children to consider the shape and colours they want to use before starting. Encourage them to change the colours as they go along, to create the effect they think is best.

SCIENCE – Cut open fruits such as kiwi, pineapple or orange and ask the children to look at the colours within them. Look carefully at the shades of one colour and the number of different colours. For example, when looking at the kiwi fruit, notice that the lines and seeds radiate from the centre, the contrasting colour of the seeds, the bright greens of the flesh and the brown skin around the edge. Use the observations as starting points for drawings.

LITERACY – Discuss with the children the things we associate with particular colours. Ask the children to 'write in colour stripes' using felt-tipped pens. For example, they may write:

Letter boxes, fire engines, danger, flames
Grass, leaves, frogs, apples, limes
Bananas, lemons, sunshine, buttercups, custard

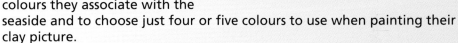

Starting with a Line

Starting points

- Ask the children what they need in order to draw a line. Challenge them to list as many ways as possible to draw a line, including using pastels, paint, chalk, pens and charcoal.

- Tell the children that you have thought of another way of drawing a line. Take a ball of very thick string or a long length of thin rope outside to a grassy or hard-surfaced area. Ask the children to help you draw a line by laying the rope on the ground as though they were drawing with a giant-sized pencil, creating shapes as the rope crosses over itself.

- Ask the children to stand in the new shapes created and see how many there are. Ask them to move the rope to change the shape in which they are standing. Do all of the shapes have curved sides?

Display

1. Provide the children with paper and thick black felt-tipped pens and ask them to create their own shapes using just one line. Ask them to try to keep the shapes fairly large. Look at the drawings together and discuss which ones they like and why.

2. Provide a large piece of paper at least 2m x 1m. Ask a child to use a pencil to create shapes using one line, covering most of the paper.

3. Ask the children to paint the shapes, keeping within the lines. When painting the shapes, you could use this as an opportunity for the children to experiment with mixing colours freely or decide on a colour theme which links into other work being covered such as 'Spring time', 'Sea and sand' or 'Light and dark'.

Further activities

- Use straight lines to create shapes. Ask the children to use a ruler and draw criss-cross lines to create shapes on a piece of A3-sized paper. Paint the shapes in shades of one colour and paint the lines black.

- Use wool to make straight lines and blocks of colour. Provide a selection of yarns and pieces of thick card or small cardboard boxes. Ask the children to wind different-coloured yarn around the card or boxes in blocks of colour, trying not to overlap the strands.

- In a safe area, on a warm day, either allocate a paving slab for each child, or draw rectangles with chalk. Ask the children to draw a line using chalk, creating shapes as they did in the main display activity. They can then colour in the shapes they have made using coloured chalks.

- Ask the children to draw shapes on paper using just one line as they as they did in the main display activity. Using pencil crayons, they can colour the shapes they have created and then draw patterns inside the shapes using felt-tipped pens.

Cross-curricular links

NUMERACY – Use ropes of different lengths to draw curved lines outside. Ask the children to tell you how they can work out which rope is the longest, without moving any of the ropes. They could measure the ropes using non-standard measures such as their feet or use a trundle wheel.

ICT – Introduce the use of the line, line style and arrow style tools. Give the children time to experiment with making patterns using arrows of different thicknesses and styles. Children who are confident about using these tools can also change the colour of the arrows and move them around the screen.

P.E. – Ask the children to make one straight line with their bodies while standing. Then ask them to move into different spiky shapes using their backs, arms, legs and fingers as straight lines, moving at the joints to change the shapes. Ask them to make the spiky shapes while lying on the floor. Use chalk to draw around the children and then talk about the shapes they have made.

What is Inside? (page 62)